NECESSARY
BUT NOT
SUFFICIENT

NECESSARY BUT NOT SUFFICIENT

A Theory of Constraints
Business Novel

Eliyahu M. Goldratt
with Eli Schragenheim and Carol A. Ptak

THE NORTH RIVER PRESS

THE NORTH RIVER PRESS
PUBLISHING CORPORATION
P. O. BOX 567
GREAT BARRINGTON, MA 01230
USA
(800) 486-2665 or (413) 528-0034

www.northriverpress.com

ISBN: 0-88427-170-6

Manufactured in the United States of
America

NECESSARY BUT NOT SUFFICIENT

Chapter 1

"Come on in" Scott stands up and shakes hands with Jay Johnstone, one of his account managers.

Calm and elegant, Scott Duncan looks more like an aristocrat than an American homegrown boy made good. At the age of 46, he heads one of the most successful computer software companies in the world.

"Have a seat." Scott gestures to the other side of his office. "I was wondering how we're doing with Alkar."

Jay lights up. Rumor has it that the nature of the discussion is indicated by on which side of Scott's office you sit. Those invited to sit in one of the chairs facing Scott's huge desk will go through a barrage of grilling, fact-finding, and an impatient string of questions. In five minutes or less you will find yourself outside the office feeling like a squeezed lemon.

But if you are guided to the other side, to one of those comfortable leather armchairs, you are likely to hear how you fit into the global picture. And there is nothing more interesting than hearing Scott Duncan unfolding the global picture. Not just his people, but now also the Wall Street analysts, are fascinated by his ability to read where businesses are heading.

Business in general, and information technology in particular. Growing his company from a modest software house into the giant it is now, with a market value of well over ten billion dollars, certainly adds a lot of credibility to what otherwise might seem as daring speculation about new technology and its impact on the market needs and trends.

As they sit down, Jay repeats Scott's question, trying to find the most concise, yet impressive answer. "How are we doing with Alkar? Well, we were one of nine companies bidding for Alkar's business. Now it's only us and FDP."

"And?"

"And it looks good."

Scott's expression causes Jay to elaborate. "We followed our standard tactic, and it's working."

If a company wants to survive in the incredibly competitive large computer system market, it has to have a lot more than just a good product. Good selling tactics are essential when the average sale is a few million dollars, and deals of several hundred million are not rare.

Scott has carved out a unique tactic for his sales force. He noticed that computer systems rapidly expand to cover more and more clerical work and that the rapid expansion is not accompanied by suitable standards. He found a way to turn this handicap of the industry into a competitive edge.

Very early in the game, preferably before the client has even put out a formal request inviting the software companies to bid, his people have already done their homework. They have identified the "techies" involved in the prospect; the people who are likely to be the ones to do the more technical evaluations of the proposed systems. These professionals become their prime target. While the competition is busy trying to locate and build bridges to the decision makers, Scott's people are busy educating these targeted professionals. Not on how the BGSoft system works, that will not do. But how in general a computer system suitable for the prospect's type of industry should be designed; the pluses and minuses of the various possible configurations; which features are key, and which ones are just good at impressing the novices.

The whole idea is that by the time the real match is reached, and the proposals are compared by the selection team for best fit, the know-how planted by Scott's people is taken as the standard. In an industry where no real standards exist, it gives Scott's company a huge advantage.

Scott looks at his computer screen, "I see that FDP was forced to add many more features into their order-entry module before a final decision could be made."

"Yes," Jay smiles. "Their first and second tries were total flops. And yesterday they had their last chance to demonstrate the process of streamlining the financial data. We were told they only succeeded in embarrassing themselves. I think that Alkar is keeping them in the race just to squeeze better terms out of us."

"How are we doing on that front?"

"Better than expected. The budget is approved and we have agreed upon the number of concurrent users. I understand that KPI Solutions has finalized the negotiations on the implementation support." Jay leans forward and softly comments, "And we still haven't used our secret weapon—the option to charge maintenance on each module separately."

With confidence he adds, "Next Monday we meet with them to finalize the details. I don't expect any real problems."

Scott smiles. He waits until Jay is looking directly at him, then he gently asks, "If it looks so good, how come in your sales report . . ." he pauses, and then continues more gently, "you estimated the probability of closing the deal this quarter at only fifty percent?"

Jay shifts uneasily in his chair. "It's only because . . ." He doesn't finish his sentence.

"You expect some surprises from FDP? Some last minute counter-attack?" Scott tries to help him.

"No, not really. My opinion is that for FDP it's too late. Nothing they come up with at this stage of the game will matter. It has nothing to do with FDP or the client, it's just . . ."

Jay is obviously uncomfortable. Then he gathers his courage, and finishes the sentence, "It's just that I thought you wanted us to be cautious."

"You mean my infamous first rule? My saying: 'be paranoid'?"

"That's right," Jay says sheepishly.

"So in your sales progress reports, that you know I read, you are trying to be paranoid?"

"Yes."

Scott leans back smiling. "Jay," he says, "if you want to mimic me, you must take into account that in my vocabulary, being paranoid means something quite different than the usual connotation. In my eyes, most people confuse being paranoid with what I call being shortsighted. Do you know how difficult it is to be truly paranoid?" He pauses as if he expects an answer.

Wisely, Jay doesn't reply.

"To be paranoid you must constantly assess the impact of your actions on the global picture. Which means that first you must relentlessly search for a deep understanding of the global picture. Do you understand?"

Jay looks unsure.

"Do you want me to explain?"

"Yes please," Jay answers eagerly. He prepares himself for something he has heard about so many times, the private conversations with this legendary CEO, conversations that will give a new dimension to how he sees the company. At least that's what everybody who was lucky enough to have the benefit of such an intimate conversation with Scott claimed.

"You have options in the company," Scott states.

"I also hold some shares." Jay volunteers the information knowing that it can only help.

"So you probably know their value?"

"This morning it was seventy-six and five-eighths. Up a little more than half a point." Jay is glad to demonstrate his local patriotism.

"I see that you are keeping track," Scott acknowledges with a nod. "Have you noticed a difference between our shares and the shares of other solid companies, like GM or GE?"

"The value of our shares is growing faster," Jay is fast to respond.

"In the last year, not by much," Scott corrects him. "I mean some other difference, one that puts us in an entirely different category than the blue chips?"

It is obvious that Jay doesn't know.

"One factor that determines the value of a company is the profit it generates," Scott patiently explains. "For most companies, the market determines their value to be between ten and twenty-five times their yearly profits. This is what is called the multiplier.

"In the eighties there was a group of companies that for a while, got high multipliers that were unprecedented. Those companies were from a new industry—genetics. At that time the impression was that fortunes could be made quickly with this new technology. Those companies were traded at multipliers as high as forty!"

Scott waits for Jay to assimilate, and then connects it back to their issue. "Do you know the multiplier that our stock trades at?"

Jay doesn't.

"Higher than a hundred!" Scott announces.

"That's excellent." Jay is enthused.

"Yes, it is," Scott agrees. "But it has its price. Why do you think the market values us so highly?"

"Because we're growing so fast?" Jay is not entirely sure.

"Correct," Scott confirms. "It's nice when a small company grows by thirty percent, from let's say three million dollars a year to four million. Nice, but nothing extraordinary. But you would hardly expect such a rate of growth from a company of thirty million dollars, and not at all from a company of three hundred million."

"But," Jay says unable to keep himself from disagreeing with his CEO. "But last year we grew from nine hundred million to . . . to . . ."

"Exactly. We have done it. We finished last year with sales of one billion, three-hundred and seventy-million. We have grown by a little over forty percent. And not just last year, but the year before, and the year before that, and the year before that."

"So the market expects that we'll do it this year as well." Jay starts to understand. Being a professional salesman, he knows that it will make a good impression to summarize his understanding. "The high multiplier that the market gives us is actually based on the expectation that we'll continue to grow at a phenomenal rate."

Scott nods in agreement, and then broadens the picture for Jay. "Our performance, good as it is, would not be sufficient to command the incredibly high multiplier of over a hundred. It is due to the confidence the market has in our industry."

Noticing that Jay doesn't get it he adds, "It's not just us, it is also our competitors. All our major competitors are growing at about the same rate. Every quarter, every single quarter, every one of the big players reports a growth rate of forty percent per year. It is now the standard in our industry. So you see Jay, it is more accurate to say that the market isn't just expecting such growth from us, the stock market is taking our incredible growth rate for granted."

Jay nods, indicating he understands.

"Having such a high multiplier," Scott continues, "is a tremendous leverage for our company. In a way it's the key to our rapid growth."

Expecting that Jay is unaware of this aspect, Scott elaborates. "In order to grow we have to constantly expand the range of products we offer the market. We are in the enviable position of not having to develop these products from scratch. We don't have to spend the time needed to develop the product and the expertise, we simply locate the best company in the field, and we buy it. For any price. You see, we don't have to pay money. Our shares are so incredibly valuable that we pay with a small fraction of them."

Scott stops and looks at Jay. "Now let's practice being paranoid. In this good situation, can you see any hidden danger?"

Jay knows, that in some way, he is now being tested. He takes his time and then says slowly, "Isn't it becoming more and more difficult to maintain such a rate of growth? I mean, now that we're over a billion, isn't it . . ."

"Yes it is. Just this morning I was telling myself that the better it is, the worse it becomes. But can you tell me what the specific danger is?"

"The market is taking for granted," Jay says, trying to do his best, "that we'll continue to grow at a rate of forty percent per year. So, if we miss our sales forecast even once . . . even by a little bit . . ." He loses his confidence, and stops.

"Very perceptive." Scott is apparently pleased. "Very good," he encourages, and then pushes for the conclusion. "What will happen then?"

Jay no longer hesitates. "I guess that the market will lose its confidence in us, and our share value will drop accordingly."

"Precisely." And then Scott modifies it a bit. "Missing the forecast on one quarter, reporting sales lower than expected, lower by let's say, thirty million dollars, would have a severe impact. My estimate is that our share value would drop by about twenty percent. God forbid we miss the forecast two quarters in a row. That will force the market to reevaluate its expectations; to speculate that the period of our rapid growth is over. In that case I would not be surprised if our shares dropped to maybe twenty percent of the current value."

Spontaneously Jay comments, "That would be a disaster."

"You can say that again," Scott agrees, and then immediately moves to negate the possibility of damaging rumors. "Luckily we are far from being in that situation." He smiles in assurance.

"So, why did I bring all of this up?" He asks.

"Because it's important," Jay answers.

"Yes. But I want you to understand the real meaning of being paranoid."

Then, Scott continues more seriously, "Being paranoid means looking and planning for the possible dangers, even in a situation that is good. Look, for example, how helpful it is in our case. An ordinary company should concentrate on maximizing profits. Since we look at the exposure for our company, we understand that for us, the prime parameter is not profit, but maintaining growth rate. That has an impact on almost everything we are doing."

Jay is silent, thinking about what he just heard. Scott waits patiently. "Now I understand," Jay mutters.

"What?"

"Now I understand what happened with my previous account. I was about to close a nice contract, over forty million dollars. What was missing was a little flexibility on the number of concurrent users. Something that we do almost on a routine basis. And then I was instructed to be firm." Jay's voice reveals how much that incident had irritated him. "True, we weren't running a real risk of losing the account, but it did cost us a delay of almost two months."

"So what insight have you gained now?"

"I guess that we already had enough that quarter, so we wanted to push the sale to the next quarter. Hmm . . ."

Scott looks at his watch. It's about time to end the conversation. "Jay, I hope that now you understand that when I say 'be paranoid,' I mean: don't be blinded by the good appearance of things, take actions to guarantee success."

"I do," Jay assures him.

Standing up, Scott casually comments, "In that light, I suggest that you examine if you are truly paranoid when you estimate only a fifty percent chance of closing a deal that is practically in the bag."

Jay smiles broadly. "I get the message."

As Scott returns to his desk he mutters to himself, "He got the message but do I get the message?"

Things are becoming tougher with every quarter. Last quarter, even though it was the end of the year, there was no safety; there were no deals that they had to defer to this year. The target is higher, the pipeline of new prospects is thinner, and what are they doing to rectify it?

Does BGSoft have a good enough strategy? A strategy that clearly shows how BGSoft will succeed in maintaining its rate of growth?

Their strategy is to do more of the same. He for one does nothing except for making sure that everything is functioning smoothly.

He is spending all his time checking. Checking the major deals that are cooking, the alignment of his key account managers, the progress of their development efforts, the quality of the service they give to their clients, the . . . The list of the details that absorb all his time is endless.

But is it enough? Is doing more of the same enough?

Chapter 2

At exactly 8:30 A.M., the electric door of the Systems Development section at HQ opens and Lenny goes inside, carrying two cups and his briefcase in a manner known only to him. The two cups, one coffee with milk, and one black tea, are also characteristic of Lenny.

Roger, VP of Systems Development, sits in his office, which is right next to Lenny's. He looks at his watch. "As usual, he's right on time," he thinks to himself. Roger is willing to bet that the date is not going to change. Lenny and Scott probably just had a nice dinner for two. Gathering up the papers on his desk, he follows Lenny into his office.

Lenny puts his cups on the table, drops his briefcase to the ground, takes a quick sip and looks up. "Good morning Roger. Before you ask, the answer is yes, April 15th is still the release date. The new vendor-performance-measures will not be included, unless I finish the detailed specs today. Any questions?"

Roger begins, "Lenny, I suggest we review, once again, the list of features going into version seven point two. The list is too long to be realistic. It's not the vendor-performance stuff.

10

I'm concerned we won't have enough time for quality assurance. Lenny, we must give our programmers clear priorities."

Lenny thinks for several seconds. "If I give you the relative importance of the new features I know what will happen. I'm not ready to give up on any of the features we've planned to include."

"Lenny, that not fair," Roger replies. "You cannot hold the stick from both sides. If you don't give us any flexibility on the release date, you must give us some leeway on the number of features."

Lenny examines Roger's face, thinks about it and says, "Okay Roger, I'll give you the priorities, just in case you do everything possible and still run out of time. But remember, I'm asking for everything. Where is the list?"

Apparently relieved, Roger hands him the list. Lenny starts to mark it.

The phone rings. Lenny doesn't bother to answer it.

The voice-mail speaker interrupts: "This is Rudy from KPI Solutions. I have a major client phasing out from MAN and coming to us. We have to show them what a cool, fast implementation we can do. Failing to convert the data can kill the implementation. I'm in a very sensitive situation here. Please call me back ASAP."

Lenny looks at Roger. "The fact that KPI Solutions gets almost all its work from us doesn't mean that we can neglect them," he says.

"You don't have to remind me that KPI is our biggest system integrator." Roger is almost insulted. "But the reality is that Phil's team is filled up with the Web-enable module that you said is priority one."

Lenny doesn't accept it. "Phil's team might be filled up with work but that doesn't mean that we can leave KPI without good service. Maybe you don't need a reminder but we depend on KPI to the same extent they depend on us. For over eighty percent of our clients, KPI Solutions is the company that implements our software."

Roger starts to describe what he is doing to compensate. "I've transferred the mission to Arthur at our office in London. He promised me a response in two weeks. I found out he assigned the job to someone named Mary. According to Arthur, she's a bright programmer—but just a kid. No real experience. So, after the first two failed attempts to do the conversion, I demanded that Arthur look at it himself. Apparently it didn't help much. So it must be a particularly nasty bug. OK, I'll ask Steve Chin to put someone good on it."

He stops, taking a deep breath.

"Why are you staring at me? I'm not going to do it myself. The last line of code I wrote was thirteen years and three months ago—I don't count the days."

Lenny smiles. "It used to be different several years ago. I remember you fixing problems like this in less than fifteen minutes."

Roger returns his smile. "You're confusing between you and me." Flatly he adds, "Some of our people are really excellent programmers, but I can't keep constantly interrupting them. The need to stop work to answer questions and fix bugs is turning their work into havoc." I'm just planning a system so clear and friendly there will be no need for questions, manuals, and help screens." Lenny says, "Come back next week and I'll show you. This really will solve all our current problems."

"What?" gasps Roger.

"Just kidding." Lenny laughs. "I find time for jokes when I'm in trouble, like now. It's my Jewish heritage. By the way, it's not such an impossible mission to write a computer system that will work right the first time. Just design a system that does nothing, and you have about a twelve percent probability it will work smoothly. In all other cases it'll do something—which means there are bugs somewhere." Porcupines have quills and programs have bugs. That's life.

Roger manages to smile. No one wishes to offend Lenny by not responding to his jokes. He likes Lenny. Everybody does, and he's too important a person to risk hurting his feelings.

Lenny finishes marking the list. Before he hands it to Roger he says, "By the way, Maggie has invited herself to discuss a document she sent me. That document shows how few of the features that KPI Solutions has requested have been authorized by me. So don't think I'm giving you too many features. Roger, here is your list. Remember, I want the release to contain *ALL* these features."

When he leaves Lenny tries to immerse himself in figuring out the technical specs for the vendor-performance requirement which he thinks is not needed in the first place. However, when a six-billion dollar company asks for something, even he has to comply. But he is trying his best to design the new feature so it won't generate any real damage. It is a challenging objective.

The door opens. Lenny continues concentrating on his work. He learned a long time ago that being busy is not enough to prevent disruptions, he must look busy. Too often people thought that when Lenny was sitting quietly looking at the ceiling, he wasn't busy. He learned his lesson and now forces himself to stare at the computer screen instead. Now people know he is really working, but even this is not enough anymore.

He keeps looking at the screen for several seconds, then raises his eyes.

"Lenny," Roger says, "there's this young French programmer. I want you to meet him."

"I'd love to, but I don't have time. Not today."

"That's what you said last week. He was sent here two months ago to work on the new display for the available-to-promise module. And I suspect that he was given the impression that he'd have the chance to work with you."

Lenny just shrugs his shoulders.

Roger tries another tact. "He thinks that there's a bug in that ATP module, and he insists on telling you about it personally."

"Did he convince you there's a bug in the ATP module?"

"Yes. As a matter of fact, I think there is a bug. He prepared a very detailed example and analysis. Quite an impressive document."

"So what's the problem? If you think it's important enough, add it to the list."

"Lenny, that's not the real issue. The thing is that the kid is really brilliant, even if he is somewhat crazy. He told me he's going home if he can't see you. And I'm concerned that he might really do it. Lenny, this is a sharp kid. We need people like that."

"OK, send the wonder child to me."

The conversation with Jean-Claude takes more than half an hour, during which time two more phone calls go into Lenny's voice mail. Lenny sees why Roger wanted him to talk with the kid. This boy has the potential to be a star. He's a programmer with a keen understanding of the use of the software, rather than simply being enchanted with the bits and bytes and features. Not to mention that he has also touched upon a logical bug that could be traced all the way to Lenny himself. Lenny appreciates people who can find flaws in his own specs.

When the phone rings, Lenny is still thinking about the ramifications of the change he'd just approved in the ATP module. He authorized the kid to fix the bug, but now wishes he'd been slower to approve it. A whole set of changes now have to be intergrated into the new version just because the bug is fixed. Sharon is not going to like it at all. The phone continues to ring and he makes the mistake of picking it up.

"Hi Lenny, this is Rudy. We have this problem at MACTEL with the conversion from MAN. We need it fixed soon. Real soon. All we need is to start with the financial module first. But there are conversion problems and we can't proceed. Roger promised that writing the conversion program would get the highest priority. But it didn't work out. Once I call up the financial module the program crashes because of bad data. This is already the third time I've received a conversion program that's supposed to work but all it does is crash. I've found the programmer who's working on it. Her name is Mary and she's part of a team in London. I called London and talked with her. Lenny, it seems to me that she doesn't have a clue."

"Rudy, I just talked with Roger about it. Give it another two days. They'll sort it out."

"I wish you would help her out, Lenny. I know you're busy with much more important and clever missions, but we're talking about a big client here that we convinced to switch from MAN to work with BGSoft. You know how much effort we put into winning over clients who work with the enemy. I'm really concerned that failing to establish our software very fast might put an end to such hopes. Please, see to the problem. I know you can remove programming obstacles within ten minutes."

Lenny likes persistent people, the bulldogs, but not when he's the target. On the other hand he doesn't want to upset Rudy with a vicious remark. Rudy was brought to KPI Solutions from Boyd and Neel. At a time when Maggie is looking everywhere for really good consultants, Lenny must be nice to such an import. Reluctantly Lenny agrees to talk with Arthur at the London office.

He bolts his door and disconnects the phone. How to integrate the vendor-performance feature is starting to shape in his mind. There is a way to sneak it in without writing hardly any additional code. But it requires small changes in many places. It will be easy if he does it himself, but quite complicated to explain it to anybody else.

Should he do it himself? Before long somebody would find out that it was not exactly what he or she needed. Changes would be demanded. At that point it would be part of the whole package, and no one would know how to do the necessary adaptations. It was just asking for trouble.

There was a time when it was so much simpler. He smiles recalling how it all started. Simply put, BGSoft owes its existence to rage, Scott's rage at the professor who gave him a mere 'C' on what Scott considered his masterpiece. The seminar was called Forecasting Future Trends. Scott, who spent his summers as an interim programmer, picked the computer industry for his project paper.

Back in 1979, the computer industry was totally dominated by the hardware companies, the companies producing the computers. There was IBM, the giant that ruled over seventy percent of the world market, and there were many smaller companies, most in the range of several hundred million dollars in annual sales. Software companies, those in the business of providing packages of computer code, were few and small. At that time a ten million dollar software company was considered large.

Two new developments had just been introduced. One was the emergence of mini-computers, which had capabilities resembling those of the huge mainframe computer. What required, just a year before, several million dollars, could now be purchased for less than two-hundred-thousand dollars. The other development was terminals, which were rapidly replacing paper punched cards as the means of communicating with the computer. These were major changes, but almost nobody foresaw that they would change the balance between the hardware and software companies. Scott did.

He had recognized that the mini-computers and terminals were removing the major obstacles standing in the way of providing a large commercial application. A small software company could now afford to own a computer. This allowed their programmers, using terminals that were directly linked to the mini-computer, to test their code dozens of times a day rather than the maximum three or four attempts that had, up until then, been possible. That, Scott concluded, would open the door to replacing the tailored, homegrown programs that companies were using with a cheaper, easier to maintain, and more powerful package that many companies could use.

Estimating that the price of hardware would continue to nose-dive, and anticipating a resulting increase in the thirst to use these powerful machines, Scott postulated in his paper that the market for large software applications would skyrocket. Alas, his professor didn't share the same opinion.

At that time, not many people were familiar with computers, so Scott had a very limited audience for airing his gripes. One of the few was Lenny, a master's student in mathematics who spent his summers in a cubical next to him.

Lenny listened and asked some questions, but his final conclusion was surprising. "Scott," he said, "you yourself don't believe in what you wrote."

In response to Scott's furious reply, he just added, "If you believe in what you wrote, don't waste time griping about your mark. Go and do it. Build a software company."

Scott raised the seed money, Lenny wrote the code, and Scott sold it. Lenny made the changes the clients demanded. And in twenty years the company grew from two people to the thousands they are now employing.

It was so easy when they could do everything themselves. His joy in finding an elegant way to easily incorporate the vendor-performance-measurement is replaced by frustration that the days of bright solutions are over. It's better to use a more cumbersome but more straightforward way. But that will be too much work. So the vendor-performance-measurement will not make it into this version. That's bad.

He is caught between a rock and a hard place. And not just on this issue but on almost everything that he is doing. That's the nature of the monstrous system that has grown here. But he is not going to solve it now. Actually he doesn't see how to solve it at all.

Maggie, the CEO of KPI Solutions, had sent him a document filled with complaints. She is coming this afternoon to discuss it and he doesn't have good news for her.

He looks at his watch. It's already past two. Lenny feels hungry. Maybe he should go down and grab something at the cafeteria. The risk is that someone with a problem could see him and start talking about this and that. No, it's better to order something to be brought to his office. And tea would be nice, too. So he calls the cafeteria and orders chicken salad, hot tea, and coffee. Then, still holding the phone, he remembers his promise to Rudy.

He calls the London office. It's a long time before the female voice answers the phone. "May I speak with Arthur please." Lenny hopes there is no other Arthur at the London office; he can't remember Arthur's last name.

"I'm sorry, Arthur has already left. There's no one in the office right now."

That's strange. Oh, it must be past seven in London.

"I assume you are in the office. Who are you?"

"I'm Mary Wittaker. I'm on Arthur's team."

"Oh, good. I actually want to talk to you. I understand you are working on the conversion program for MAN, and that there's some problem with it?"

The line is silent for several long seconds.

"Who is talking, please?"

"This is Lenny Abrahms."

The line is silent again.

"Mary, it's all right. I used to be a programmer. I just thought we could discuss the nature of the bug. You see, the people working with MACTEL are somewhat nervous, and they understand nothing about programming. So I thought maybe I could help."

It takes Mary some time to calm herself and talk with 'The Big Lenny.' After about fifteen minutes, during which time somebody knocked on his door, Lenny succeeds in tracing the source of the bug to the Bill-of-Material data structure.

"That can't be it," Mary exclaims. "I've checked that code three times already." She suddenly feels frightened. You're not supposed to say 'it cannot be' to Lenny.

"Check again. It has to be there. All the signs lead to it." The banging on the door resumes.

"Sorry, I have to go now. Check it Mary, I still have a good nose for bugs."

The bangs grow louder. Lenny opens his door. He forgot he

had bolted it. Lenny's secretary is standing there with the waiter from the cafeteria, holding a tray.

"Sorry you disconnected the phone."

There is no free spot on the desk. Lenny signals the waiter that it's perfectly all right to put the tray on a pile of papers.

"You don't have too much time," his secretary reminds him.

You are supposed to meet Maggie at Scott's office. And that meeting starts in less than ten minutes.

"OK, I'll just taste the salad and go. I'm too aggressive when I'm starving and it is not a good idea to be aggressive with Maggie."

Three minutes later, Lenny heads to Scott's office.

Chapter 3

"We were late by seven months, we haven't yet successfully installed the sale's configurator, and you're telling me that we still won the Osboron contract?" Scott tries to digest. Then he sarcastically concludes, "Our competitors must be in really bad shape."

"That's one plausible explanation," Maggie grins. "Another one is Y2K. If it weren't for the pressure it's putting on Osboron to decide, I don't think that anybody would have won."

Scott laughs. "If the year two thousand didn't exist, we should have invented it. This bug gave a tremendous lift to our industry. We are lucky."

More seriously he adds, "But we both know that luck had nothing to do with it. We're getting the contract because our people worked day and night. I know that Osboron was a particularly demanding client with many unique demands, but Maggie, were we exceptionally late in supplying the new features that we had committed to?"

"Frankly, every single one was quite late. And my team could do with fewer bugs. But what's important is that your people did deliver the code. And that at last, we got most of the weird features to work."

"So you are satisfied with the current performance?"

"Far from it," Maggie firmly denies. "We have a problem here. A serious problem that is rapidly growing."

"That is also my impression," Scott agrees. "Have you discussed it with Roger?"

"Constantly. He tries his best, but the guy is just VP of software development. I'm afraid that what we are facing here is beyond his ability to solve."

"That's what you want to talk to Lenny about?"

"Exactly. We have a meeting in . . ." she glances at her watch, "in less than thirty minutes. I sent him my analysis two days ago. We must find a good enough way to stop the deterioration. Quickly."

What deterioration? Scott wonders to himself. Scott knows that Maggie would not use such strong words if she were only referring to bugs in the system.

Maggie lives at a fast pace. Although often a bit abrupt with people she knows well, she is really a very nice person. Her thick red hair gives her a sporty appearance, and she has a tall, elegant profile.

Her warm smile and flashing green eyes have fooled more than one businessman, Scott recalls. She is one serious lady, and a damn hard worker. Whatever the problem, Lenny and Maggie should be able to work it out. He has to deal with other problems. Like the difficulty of getting enough sales. He suspects that it is not a temporary problem, but rather a threat he has to deal with. Still, problems in implementation can effect every other aspect of the business.

He makes up his mind. "Do you mind if we move your meeting with Lenny here?"

"On the contrary."

Scott walks to the door, "Mary-Lou, can you ask Lenny if it's all right to have his meeting with Maggie in my office?"

Turning back to Maggie he says, "In the meantime, can I hear a little bit more about the Osboron deal?"

"Fine, back to Osboron. As I told you, last week the pilot implementation we did in the light aircraft division was finally presented to their evaluation team. Yesterday, they decided not to wait any longer for FDP or Data Storm, and to make our system the standard for the entire corporation. This morning I confirmed that I will personally meet them next Monday to go over the required changes to the proposal we submitted two years ago."

With all the problems and frequent delays the implementation team has had for the last two years in that pilot, Scott thinks to himself, it's no wonder sales gave it a low probability, even for next quarter.

"How big is your cut?" Scott asks Maggie.

"Almost twice the size of yours," she grins at him. "They won't get away with paying KPI Solutions less than ninety million."

"That means you'll have to put fifty more people in there." When it comes to numbers, Scott's brain works like a computer. He's already calculated that the Osboron deal is sufficient for him to close the quarter nicely. He can wait until after Maggie leaves to check the exact figures.

"About fifty," Maggie agrees. "We're prepared for it."

"I don't know how you do it," Scott comments. "We have the luxury of hiring programmers all over the world. They don't even have to relocate here. You know that today almost half of our programming is done in our center in India. But you have much less flexibility. To service your clients in France, for example, you need people who not only know the language, but are part of the French culture."

"Right. It is my number one priority to get enough people without compromising on their quality. You know how much I have invested in putting together a head-hunting network."

"Not really. How much?"

"Whatever it takes." Maggie is determined. "This problem is

just going to intensify. You are lucky. After a contract is signed, the client doesn't absorb a lot of your people's time. For me, it's the opposite. My people work alongside yours until we get the contract, but then I have to pour many more people in, and they are stuck there working for the next two or three years."

"Stuck there for two thousand dollars a day!" Scott teases.

"That's not the point," she argues. "The point is that we sell almost double what we did two years ago, so for each person who is released from a completed implementation, I need two or more to deliver on the new implementations. I've made a calculation that even if you continue to sell only at the present rate, which I know is unrealistic, I will still need to recruit at least . . ."

"Hi!" Lenny enters Scott's office and joins them.

"Exactly the person I wanted to see." Maggie turns toward him.

"Hi, Lenny," Scott greets him. "Maggie, before you start shooting at Lenny, can we finish what we were just talking about? You were saying that this year you'll have to recruit, how many people?"

"At least two thousand more. And a major part of the problem is you, Lenny."

"That's a relief." Lenny doesn't seem to be overly concerned. "After being accused all day of being *THE* problem, it's nice to hear that for at least one person, I'm just 'a part of the problem.' Thank you Maggie." He bows in her direction, and takes a seat.

She smiles at him. "Did you get the analysis I sent you?"

"Yeah. It doesn't look good," Lenny answers.

"Can you fill me in?" Scott asks.

"With pleasure," Lenny smiles. "Big headaches we're always glad to share with you. Maggie, you brought it up, you start."

"It ties into what we've been discussing just now," Maggie begins. "KPI Solutions is stretched. I have a chronic shortage of good people. So, since I don't have people to spare, I was looking to see how I could more effectively use the people that I already have. Look what I found."

Maggie opens her briefcase and hands Scott two colored pages. "This graph shows, month by month, the average response time of your tech-support centers."

The graph is alarming. Two years ago the response time to KPI questions was, on average, three days. Now it has deteriorated to almost ten days.

"Now look at the next graph. It shows you the response time for the last quarter. You can see that ten percent took over three weeks to answer. Those are the killers. Lenny, Scott, we knew that the situation was not good, but did you know it was this bad?"

"No, we didn't," Scott says, walking to his desk. "What I am told is that the average response time of our support centers has remained at less than twenty minutes. But that's for all questions, including the vast majority from users who have never read the manuals."

He grabs the mouse. A few clicks and he announces, "The response time to KPI questions. Here it is. It doesn't even resemble your data."

He thinks for a second. "Maggie, how are you defining response time from our support centers?"

"It's very straightforward. When a problem is identified as one that we need your input on, we log the time we call the support center. It remains open until the answer we get fixes the problem."

"That explains the discrepancy," Lenny says. "Our support centers log a response time from question to answer—not as KPI is monitoring us, from question to correct answer." After a slight pause he adds, "I agree that your way is much more meaningful."

"Let me tell you," Maggie continues, "in most cases the first answer we get is worthless. To get a better answer takes much longer; the rookies you put on the phones have to contact somebody who knows something. But surprise, surprise, many of the answers we get at the second go-round are also worthless. Lately there are cases when we have to go back and forth half a dozen times."

Lenny doesn't contradict her.

"This wastes my people's time more than anything else. We can live with bugs if we can get a quick fix, or at least a quick work-around. But it becomes impossible when my people have to spend weeks until they get an intelligent fix."

"Not to mention the friction it constantly injects between our organizations," Lenny agrees.

"And the ramifications it has on elongating the implementations and the resulting damage to both our companies' reputations," Maggie adds.

"What are we going to do about it?" Scott asks Lenny.

"Wait. It's bad, I know. But it becomes much worse. Maggie, show him the next problem."

Maggie picks up another page, but doesn't hand it over.

"In the last six years the implementation of the software has played a larger and larger role in BGSoft's business. One might think that BGSoft would be more and more responsive to KPI's requests. Especially when these requests are initiated with only one thing in mind, making your clients happy with your software."

"Isn't that the case?" Scott is alarmed.

"I'm sure we get preferred treatment," Maggie smiles.

"So why are you pulling my leg?"

"I just want to stress a point. What I'm going to show you does not represent your company's responsiveness to the market in general. It represents BGSoft's responsiveness to its preferred systems-integrator. So the overall picture is even gloomier. Now, here's the harsh reality that we have to live with." She hands Scott the page.

Maggie explains the graph. "Six years ago, when KPI spun off from BGSoft, you gave us whatever we asked for. Every new feature we requested, we got. Maybe not as fast as we wanted, but we got it. About three years ago, BGSoft introduced a new rule. Every request for a feature had to be approved. I thought it was ridiculous. What do you think, that we ask for features the client doesn't demand?"

Before Lenny has a chance to interject she continues, "I didn't really care, because as you can see from the graph, over eighty percent of our requests were fulfilled. And yes, some of our requests were because of a whim on the part of of my people. But look what happened since then. It has continued to deteriorate.

"Scott, did you know that less than twenty percent of our requests for new features are approved? Less than twenty percent!"

After a moment of silence, Maggie says, "I don't know what's worse, this problem, or the one I showed you before."

"Neither," Lenny says.

He raises his hand to prevent them from jumping to the wrong conclusion. "I've been thinking about it since I received your analysis Maggie. And the problem is much bigger than we think.

"As you know there is only one person, in all of BGSoft, who is authorized to approve a new feature, no matter how large or small it is. And that person is . . . me.

"Maggie, do you think that I approve only twenty percent of your people's requests because I think that they don't know what they're asking for? Or that I completely don't trust their judgment? Or that I've decided to go on some suicidal power trip?"

"Scott wouldn't let you. So Lenny, what *is* going on?"

"We're caught between a rock and a hard place. And they're closing in on us."

They wait for an explanation. But Lenny gets up and walks away. His back to them, he stares out the window.

"Lenny?"

He doesn't turn around. "I'm not happy with my conclusion, so I'd rather have you think about it independently."

"Maggie, it seems that we have two alternatives. We can try

torturing him for an explanation, or we can try to figure it out ourselves. You want to choose?"

Maggie smiles. "Frankly, right now I tend toward the torture, but it's too much work. So let's give solving it a try. Where do we begin?"

"I'd start with the fact that your analysis triggered Lenny to reach his conclusion."

"That sounds reasonable. What new information did my analysis give Lenny?" She thinks for a moment and then says, "Since he's the one who approves requests for new features, it's unlikely my analysis gave him any new ideas on that point."

"Correct," Scott agrees. "But I believe that Lenny was as surprised as I was to discover the extent of poor service our tech centers give your people. Three weeks response time on over ten percent of the problems that they encounter is totally unacceptable."

"Agreed. So where do we take it from here?"

"Let's put ourselves in Lenny's shoes," Scott suggests. "He's the one who determined the procedures governing the tech centers operations. As a matter of fact, less than a year ago, he spent a lot of time reorganizing Technical-Support almost from scratch. Knowing Lenny's capabilities, it seems unlikely that this reorganization is what caused the deterioration."

"So what did cause it?"

"Maggie, I think you hit the nail on the head. Your question is probably the core question. Lenny. Hey Lenny! What do you think is the main reason for the long response time of our support centers? Come on, you're the only one who really knows what's going on there."

Reluctantly Lenny rejoins them. "Isn't it obvious?" he mutters. He looks from one to the other. "Our ERP system became too complex."

The full meaning of what Lenny is saying starts to dawn on them as he continues. "I can still remember a time when each programmer knew all the modules. Now I don't even think that I know them. Actually I don't think that there is one person who knows even a single module inside and out. The monster has become too big, too complex."

His voice becomes tense as he continues. "That has numerous serious ramifications."

He starts to list them. "It takes much longer to design how to best incorporate a new feature. Since a programmer has only a rudimentary understanding of the program structure, every single feature that he programs creates at least three new bugs somewhere else. Our quality assurance starts to be a bad joke. The system contains so many possible routes that it's virtually impossible to track and check them all.

"I'm not surprised that many of the questions take us a long time to respond. I should have predicted it. Years ago, it was easy to trace the source of a bug and fix it. Today the software is complex to the extent that there are many plausible ways to explain the existence of a malfunction, and at the same time the know-how of the best programmer is not sufficient to narrow down the possibilities. They have to check them all, and that takes time. A lot of time."

"So not only do we have more bugs," Scott summarizes, "but it also takes much longer to fix each one of them."

"Exactly," Lenny confirms. "Now look at our support centers. Maggie, you called the people who man the phones rookies. Let me tell you, they are anything but. Each one of them is an experienced programmer who went through a grueling training for several months to understand the system and how it operates. They are, probably, the people with the best overall understanding of BGSoft."

"So are my people," Maggie interjects. "And yes, you're right. It takes longer and longer to bring new recruits up to speed."

"Precisely. KPI does give their people excellent overview knowledge. So when your people call, there is a good chance that the knowledge will not be contained in the standard tech-support database, and that it requires knowledge that exists only in the development departments. Even starting with a good description of the problem, it's not easy to trace which part of the code contains the bug. And as I said before, once you correctly identify the block of code, it is still a lot of work to pinpoint the bug and fix it properly."

"That explains the horrendously long response time to urgent problems," Scott concludes. "Lenny, do you think that we made a mistake in adding so many modules to our system?"

"No," Lenny answers confidently. "If we want to stay competitive we must broaden the scope our system covers. We must have more modules. And the number of modules is not the problem. It is still a manageable number, and the interfaces between them are well defined. I'm making sure of that. The problem is the numerous features each module contains. By now, many modules have become monstrous." Decisively he says, "The features are the killer."

"That's why you're so careful when approving new ones." Scott states more than asks.

Lenny nods. "Yes. There was a time I was convinced that the rapid increase in the number of features was a temporary phenomenon. Once we had included enough of them, we would be able to cover any plausible desire of our clients, and then the system would stabilize.

"I don't believe that any more. It looks like the imaginations of our clients do not have boundaries. It's true that in the last twelve months, in spite of tremendous pressure, I approved less than half of the requests for new features. Nevertheless, if you look at the absolute numbers, you'll find that the number of new features that we did incorporate is three times the number that we incorporated in the previous twelve months. Today, my opinion is that the user friendliness of our system, and the flexibility that it radiates, encourages users to ask for more tailored features. It will keep on growing."

He pauses for a moment and then adds with a sigh, "Still, I fully agree with Maggie. We cannot stay in business if we respond to only twenty percent of our client's wishes for new features."

"We are truly between a rock and a hard place," Maggie assents. "In order to bring service back to an acceptable level, we must simplify the system. But in order to respond to the market needs, we must keep on complicating it. Lenny, what are we going to do?"

"I don't know. The better our system becomes, the worse it is." Strange, Scott thinks to himself. That same sentence keeps flashing in my mind. But I am thinking about the sales aspect. Do the two problem relate? Are they two separate problems, or just two faces of the same problem?

Maggie breaks into his thoughts when she asks Lenny, "When do you think it will blow up in our face?"

"It is blowing up in our face."

Scott remarks, "The only thing that prevents the current situation from affecting our sales is that our competitors are caught in the same mess, and the market still perceives our product as bringing more value than hardship."

"Some consolation," Maggie comments.

"Look Maggie, I'm not a magician," Lenny responds. "I racked my brain to find a solution. All I can offer is something that will hopefully delay further deterioration for a while."

"You mean version eight that we plan to release six months from now?" Scott asks.

"Eight months," Lenny is quick to correct him. "Version eight is a complete restructuring of the entire system that will make it easier to understand, operate, and maintain. But I must warn you, at the rate that I see things moving, in less than a year we'll find ourselves right back where we are today.

"I no longer believe that there is a technical solution to our dilemma. Not within the existing technology. Scott, you persuaded me that any dilemma has a simple and powerful solution. That to find it you just have to expand the scope of the area you're looking at. The problem is, I don't know what can possibly be a bigger scope than our entire system."

"There is a broader scope, Lenny. The computer system is just one component in our game. There is also us as a company, the implementers, and the clients. To find a solution, maybe we'll have to look at the global picture."

"Good," says Lenny. "Consider the ball in your court."

Chapter 4

Luckily, it is perfect spring weather. Gail, the Vice President of marketing and sales for BGSoft, glances around. After the long day of presentations everybody was so happy to be outside. The din of three hundred salespeople talking, all at once—even outside—is amazing. Nothing can stop a salesperson from talking. Surely not another salesperson, which just provokes them to talk louder. A blast of smoke from one of the huge barbecue pits sends her off toward fresh air.

Smiling left and right, she picks up a glass of wine from a waiter. Gail surveys the crowd. The mood is up; the day has been good. Overall, anyway.

But where is Scott? The crowd spills off the large porch, down two levels of terraces, and onto the lawn. She sees the team from Australia looking like they're about to pull some prank. God, and it's still so early. She quickly looks away.

She can't spot Scott. His height usually makes him easy to pick out of a crowd, but . . .

"Gail!" She smiles and exchanges a hug with Brad. He's been with BGSoft for quite a while. She sincerely likes him—these are the best type of business buddies.

"Great sessions today. How come Lenny didn't come up with this great architecture sooner?" he teases, his eyes twinkling.

Someone touches her arm. "Gail, I'd like to introduce Sean."

"Carole, how nice to see you." She can't remember who Sean is.

"Hello," she smiles at him, shaking hands. Smiling is easy. His mischievous Irish grin is infectious.

"Miss Collins." He bows his head. " 'Tis an honor, I'm sure."

"This is just great!" Brad interrupts. "You know, we work so hard, the travel, the trade shows. We have to fence with the competition and then dance to please the customers. I know I come to these corporate shindigs ready to air my gripes . . . and then Lenny does one of his magic shows and . . . well, all I can say, once again, is, I'm so gung ho about BGSoft!"

The Irishman nods, "Seriously, the competition is going to eat our dust."

People are beginning to line up by the barbecue pits. She feels a familiar firm grip on her shoulder. She turns.

"How does the queen of the ball feel?" Scott greets her.

"Scott, I was looking for you," she begins.

"I'm flattered," he grins.

"Have you noticed the reaction to Lenny's presentation?" Gail asks.

"Yes. And I must admit that it's too enthusiastic for my taste."

"I should have known something like that wouldn't escape you. Did you also figure out why everybody is so enthusiastic?"

"Not exactly," Scott admits. "When can you fill me in?"

"Tomorrow morning, first thing?"

"In case you've forgotten, at breakfast I'm speaking to this fine sales force you've gathered here." He keeps smiling and nodding hello to people passing them, all heading to the buffet lines.

"Scott, it's not just important, it is urgent, we must meet before the day starts." Her tone of voice contradicts her beaming expression.

He looks at her with slight surprise, "Okay then. Seven o'clock? Hello Gunter, Nice to see you."

They drift apart, doing what they are supposed to do—making themselves available.

Now Gail has to convince Lenny to be at that early-bird meeting. That won't be too hard, she knows exactly which buttons to press. But first, she has to find him. She heads toward the nearest large group.

Scott opens the door. Room service? Oh yes, Gail probably ordered coffee for them. But why so many cups? Before he even signs the slip, Lenny arrives.

"Got tea here?" he asks.

They glance at the tray. It's there.

Lenny finishes pouring himself a cup of tea and reaches for the coffee pot. "Scott, there is no way that I'm moving the release date of version eight forward."

"Who asked you to?"

"Isn't that the purpose of this meeting?"

The picture starts to form in Scott's mind. Laconically he answers, "We'd better wait for our Machiavelli."

As if on cue, there is a knock. He opens the door.

"Good morning," Gail greets them as she walks in.

"If you say so," Lenny snaps. "Gail, before you get started, I want to make one thing clear. This time I'm not going to yield to any pressure. The release date of version eight is firmly set for October First and nothing—nothing at all that you might bring up—will change it."

"I'm just asking you to listen."

"No way, Gail." Lenny is determined. "This time you listen to me. Do you realize what version eight is?" he asks rhetorically. "It's a complete shuffle of the internal structure of each and every module. We are changing the entire architecture of the system."

"Yes, Lenny. I listened to everything you said yesterday. And I loved every word."

"You still aren't listening." Lenny starts to sound desperate. "Do you know how many possible bugs such a change creates? Gail, this version is unlike anything we've done before. It isn't simply a matter of writing a lot of additional code. It's much more involved. We are going through almost every piece of code, and making many small, but important changes. It's like massive brain surgery. If we don't devote enough time to do thorough quality assurance, we won't just be releasing a system with bugs, we'll be releasing a disaster."

"I understand," Gail says calmly.

Scott examines her. "You understand, but you still want to release version eight earlier?" he speculates.

"That's correct." Gail is firm. "We need this version no later than July first."

"What?" Lenny almost jumps to his feet.

Scott puts his hand on his shoulder. "Calm down, Lenny. Gail would not make such a preposterous demand unless she had an alarming reason for it."

Gail looks at Lenny and says, "'Alarming' is a fair description."

"What is it?" Lenny's tone is calmer but still aggressive.

Gail turns to Scott. "Last quarter was the first time in years that I had to really worry about not meeting the forecast."

"I told you that the Osboron deal would come through," Scott interjects.

"Yes, and luckily it did. But you know that we were sailing too close to the wind. For the first time ever, we didn't have any backup."

Scott nods.

"Well, it looks like this quarter we're in a much worse situation. From what I see right now, we are going to be short at least a hundred million. I don't see any way to meet the sales targets besides doing what we both always objected to. We must make large concessions to push forward some major deals."

"That is bad."

"That's very bad," Gail agrees. "Because it will ruin our chances of meeting the forecast for the next quarter."

"To that extent?" Lenny is apparently surprised.

"Yes," Scott confirms. "Our pipeline of prospects is getting thinner. Pushing some major deals forward will create too big a hole down the road."

"Why is our pipeline in such poor shape?" Lenny wonders aloud.

Scott and Gail are looking at each other, but no one volunteers an answer.

That makes Lenny even more nervous. "Are we losing our position in the market? To whom?"

"To no one," Gail answers.

"So what is going on? How come all of a sudden we're facing such a crisis?" Lenny is upset. In a sharp tone he asks Gail, "Can I get some answers?"

Before Gail has a chance to answer, Scott interjects in a calm voice. "Lenny, it has nothing to do with our marketing or sales. They continue to do an excellent job. Finding someone to blame is not the way to solve a problem."

"You're right," Lenny admits. He finishes his coffee, then picks up his cup of tea and leans back. "As the cliché says, when you are in a hole, stop digging," he jokes. "Now that I'm somewhat calmer, can I hear what's actually going on?"

"It's something that we should have predicted a long time ago," Scott starts to explain. "Still, I'm embarrassed to say that I myself didn't even suspect it until it almost hit us in the face."

"Maybe you should be more paranoid," Lenny mocks.

"That's what I keep on reminding myself," Scott smiles back.

"Can you lay it on me in one sentence?" Lenny prods, reminding Scott that he's anxious to know what's going on.

"There are not enough deer left in the forest."

Lenny looks puzzled. "Okay you two, lay it on me in as many sentences as you like."

Gail looks at Scott. He signals that he will explain.

"As you know, over eighty-five percent of our revenues come from large companies, companies which have over a billion dollars in annual sales. There is a limited number of such big companies."

Understanding starts to spread over Lenny's face. "How many of these companies have already bought an ERP system?" he asks.

"Over eighty percent."

"So many? So you're telling me, that in our main market, we're reaching saturation?"

"Yes," Scott confirms.

Gail doesn't look as if she agrees, but before she has a chance to object, Lenny offers a suggestion. "If there are not enough deer left, then we'd better start shooting rabbits. The market of midsize companies is far larger than the market of big companies."

"Yes," Scott agrees. "The midsize market, companies with annual sales of over a hundred million, is at least ten times larger than the large companies market." Seeing how uncomfortable Gail is, he continues, "But there are some problems with it. Gail?"

"Calling it 'some problems' is the understatement of the year," Gail snorts. "We have quite a bit of experience selling to the mid-market. If you think that it's any easier to sell to a five-hundred-million dollar company, think again. The sales cycle takes about as long, somewhere between six and eighteen months. And the efforts to make the sale are almost the same. The only thing that's different is the money that we see at the end. That's not the same at all.

"Do you realize what it would take to generate four-hundred-million dollars in sales from mid-market clients? In each quarter we would need to close deals with something like three hundred companies. I don't have the people."

"Eventually, though, we'll have to go there," Scott remarks.

"Eventually maybe, but not now," Gail says decisively.

"Right now we don't have a large enough sales force, and much more importantly, we don't have the time."

Scott and Lenny look at each other. To emphasize her last point, Gail says, "We have the problem on our door step. Maybe we can manage this quarter, but it is unrealistic to expect a three-fold increase in our mid-market sales for next quarter. It's totally unrealistic."

"So, what do you suggest?" Scott asks.

"I don't agree with you that the market of large companies is saturated. Not for another year at least. I'm not talking about the still significant number of companies that have not yet bought an ERP system. I'm talking about two major markets. One is our own clients. We tend to forget the fact that just because they bought our system doesn't always mean that we can't get additional large sales from them."

"You mean additional modules?" Lenny inquires.

"No. As you know, our price is based on number of users. For many of our clients the number of users is appalling. Take for example Sitburg Industries. This company has over a hundred-and-fifty-thousand employees, but they have only six thousand users. I think we can do a lot there to encourage much higher usage of our system."

"That's not going to be easy," Scott comments.

"Nothing in our business is easy," Lenny replies, "but we thrive on the difficult."

"That's right. And our development can thrive on the difficult task of providing version eight in three months," Gail says, grabbing the opportunity.

"Forget it," Lenny says flatly.

"Gail, you haven't yet told us why it's so important to move the release date up," Scott reminds her.

"There's another big opportunity that is now opening wide," Gail starts to explain. "You know that many ERP implementations are floundering. Four years of effort without seeing the end of the implementation in sight is not rare. As can be expected, companies that have found themselves in this situation are not happy. There are threats of litigation in the air."

"You call that an opportunity?" Lenny questions.

"Definitely," Gail declares confidently. "Since the beginning of the year we have been working on identifying companies that are sick and tired of their ERP vendor. So far we have located at least a dozen that we think might be ready to change. What we need is an excellent pitch, something to convince them that they will not go through the same fiasco with us. And Lenny, we heard such a pitch. Yesterday. From you."

"That's why your sales force is so encouraged by Lenny's presentation." Scott has his confirmation.

"Exactly. Everyone who is out there trying to sell knows that the battle field has changed. The war is no longer on options and configurations. It's about speed of implementation. It's about simplicity and ease of installation. And that is exactly what Lenny was talking about. Not just talking, but proving that our system contains everything and is still simple. Showing exactly how it's achieved. It was convincing. It was beautiful. Exactly what we need."

"And it still can't be done before September." Lenny tries to pour cold water on Gail's enthusiasm.

It doesn't work.

"Lenny, you've performed miracles before. I trust you."

Scott puts his hand on Lenny's shoulder to prevent him from commenting, and asks Gail, "Suppose that we had version eight right now. When do you think you could bring in more sales?"

"Within two to three months I can bring an additional one hundred million. Maybe more. We have all the lines in the water. The fish are desperate. What we need is good bait. That's all."

Keeping his hand on Lenny's shoulder, Scott continues, "And if we announce that we're ready to accept beta tests starting the first of July?"

Gail answers, "Make it June first and it will help to push

some of the mature prospects over the hump. As a matter of fact, it might solve our problem for this quarter. But Scott, this will not help at all with the real dilemma. The companies that I'm talking about, those who might be ready to change vendors, will not even consider testing. They've had more than their fill of tests. They want something solid."

Scott turns to Lenny. "Most of the code is ready, isn't it?"

Lenny knows that he is now fighting a losing battle, but he still tries. "Yes, but that's not the issue. The quality assurance is the problem."

"And if you go to India to personally supervise the efforts?"

Lenny looks as if he has just swallowed a particularly bad-tasting frog.

"Lenny, it's our only choice," Scott says in his deep voice. "The alternative is to miss the forecast, one quarter after another. And you know what that means. Gail is right, September is much too late. We have to come out with version eight no later than July. June is much better. And we have to announce it to our sales force. Today. Every day counts."

Lenny looks sick, but he manages to mutter, "India, here I come."

Chapter 5

Maggie, being a first class passenger, is one of the first to board the airplane. Waiting for Scott to arrive she reviews the notes that her implementation team had given her just before leaving the office.

Maggie's project manager, George, had reported only minor difficulties in the implementation project, but nothing significant enough to warrant a summons to appear in person. The project is on schedule and on budget—what could be wrong? Compared to a number of other projects where time or budget or both were doubled before the project was over, this is a real success in the making. It had better be! Maggie hand-selected George for this particular job because she and Scott had personally sold it. George has been with her longer than any other consultant. His strong background as a successful practitioner made him an excellent consultant.

A successful implementation here would surely leverage more business for both her and Scott. A strong reference from a very large company with a recognized name goes a long way in selling to companies lower down the Fortune 1000 list.

As she expected, Scott takes his seat, well before the door is closing.

After they reach cruising altitude, and the airplane engines idle down, the two begin to talk about the strange call she received from Craig yesterday. Craig is CEO of Pierco, one of their largest customers. His request was so urgent that they both agreed to clear their calendars and take the first flight this morning. Craig did not go into any details during the call, but they both know that such urgency cannot possibly be good news.

"What did your people tell you about Pierco's implementation?" Maggie starts to compare notes. "How many bug reports and feature requests are still open outstanding?"

"Craig didn't call us both over there just for some minor programming tweaks and questions." Scott brushes her question aside. And then half jokingly he adds, "So it must be about your project team. Have you overcharged them for something? More than usual, I mean."

Maggie smiles and quickly responds, "That last upgrade, with all the goodies that you promised Pierco, sure made us scramble. But we still got it installed in time to support the Pierco conference room pilot on schedule last month. You would think that with that release being three months late it would have worked when we got it. We spent a significant amount of overtime, which we didn't even bill for, to fix all the bugs that we found when we tried to use it."

"Now that I think of it, I should send you a bill for that," Maggie jokingly adds.

The flight attendant interrupts. "Would you like the cereal or the omelet for breakfast?"

"Cereal and black coffee," Maggie replies.

More implementations and increasing project complexity require her to travel more than ever before. The hectic routine is beginning to show in her waistline. She had better start being careful or none of her expensive suits will fit anymore. She learned to splurge on new clothes when she was promoted to head the BGSoft implementation division six years ago. That was just before KPI Solutions was spun off as a separate company. At the time, the new clothes were more than she could really afford, but if you are going to be successful, you have to look successful. And looking successful requires constant investment. Still, shopping was something that she did not enjoy. Maggie is glad she has somebody to take care of that for her now.

"Seriously Scott," she picks up the conversation. "Thank God for Lenny. Without him, I don't think it would be running yet. I myself had to put some pressure on him because I know that when he gets personally involved, the work gets done. I know, I know, he's busy with version eight. Too bad your other programmers can't seem to figure it out without him. If they could, then the software would work right the first time."

"There is no such person," Scott says flatly. "And I don't think that Craig called us in to talk about trivial things like the conference room pilot or the latest release, either. Something must be very wrong. Maybe one of your macho consultants did something that offended Craig's people?"

Maggie shakes her head again, "KPI Solutions people are too professional for that. If I hired kids straight from college, I would expect some difficulty until they learned how to act in the business world. However, my people are all experienced professionals." She grins at him. "Besides, I checked. It must be something else."

Maggie continues, "Craig is never that abrupt on the telephone. Usually he talks about his golf game, his wife and the kids first, but this time he went directly to the point and asked to see both of us—personally. He really has me wondering what this is all about."

No closer to an answer about what they would find when they arrived at Pierco; they both opened their laptops. One good thing about flights, you can catch up on backlogged e-mail.

Their driver meets them at the gate and they are soon out of the airport and on the familiar route to Pierco. When they arrive,

Craig's secretary immediately accompanies them to his office. He is behind his huge desk, but quickly moves to welcome them. Craig tells his secretary to hold all his calls, he wants no interruptions.

He's a big man and when he shakes Maggie's hand, her hand totally disappears into his. Maggie never feels totally comfortable around him. He's always impeccably dressed and groomed, right out of the pages of GQ. Always in control of everything. And although he has a slight smile on his face, Maggie knows him well enough to see that today he is tense.

"How good to see you again, Maggie. How was your flight?"

Then, turning to Scott, "It has been a while, old man. How is business for you? I see your name in the journals from time to time. Have a seat."

They sit down. Craig doesn't. He starts to pace around his office. "You are probably both wondering why I called you in on such short notice. I do appreciate that you were both able to clear your schedules and get here so quickly. I need your help."

Maggie smiles and responds, "I must admit that we have been wondering."

Craig nods and says, "Well, you see, I had my board of directors meeting yesterday. To say it was not pleasant would be an understatement. I cannot remember any other instance when I was chewed up so badly. And for no real reason."

This does little to clarify for Scott and Maggie the real reason for their presence here. Craig is not the type who looks for sympathy.

"I have a new director on the board," Craig continues. "A young, aggressive fellow who thinks the way to make an impression is by rocking the boat. And he picked your project as the target. At the meeting before last, he raised the concern of so many companies experiencing huge budget overruns on their ERP implementations. He quoted from a survey, case by case, where companies had paid hundreds of millions of dollars more that they had originally planned. I assured him that we are not one of them, and that I would report in more detail at the next board meeting, which was yesterday."

Maggie interrupts, "That should have been a short briefing since the project is on time and on budget."

"Exactly. Actually," Craig winks, "it wasn't so short, since the project, thanks to you, is running smoothly, and I wanted to show off. Well, this little weasel let me go through all the details. When I finished, he dropped his bomb. In his squeaky voice he asked only one question, one which has been echoing inside my head since then.

"I'll quote him verbatim: 'You have invested three-hundred-and-twenty million dollars of this company's money in this project, what can you show us for all that money?'"

Craig stops. There is an awkward silence in the room. He takes a deep breath and continues, "All the board looked at me to answer. As if they had nothing to do with this project. As if they weren't the ones who pushed me into it and approved it. And I was left sitting there not knowing how to answer."

His tone hardens. "I called you here because I still don't know what the answer is." Craig stresses his last point with his huge hand, flat to the table. Just the size of his hands makes the noise louder than expected.

"I don't understand." Maggie is apparently confused. "What can be such a problem? This project has had a solid business justification right from the beginning. I would think all the acquisitions you have done since have only strengthened the justification. Isn't that so?"

"Maggie, when the banner is 'what can you show for it,' and everybody around the table takes that to mean 'show us on the bottom line,' the hard dollar return, then most items in our fine business justification somehow evaporate into thin air."

"I still don't understand," Maggie insists. Turning to Scott, she asks, "Do you?"

"I'm not sure," Scott admits.

"Look," Craig says. "On the original business justification

that you helped us with we had, for example, an item indicating a benefit like—'better visibility into operations.'"

Maggie interjects, "I'm sure that at the time the board was asked to approve the project, 'better visibility into operations,' was a strong argument."

"Correct," Craig confirms. "But so what?"

"I suspect," Scott says, "that this board meeting was not the appropriate forum to show what better visibility actually boils down to. To present the entire data flow; how the computer system actually integrates all of it. How when an order is entered in one of the sales offices, the . . ."

Craig doesn't let him finish. "Scott," he says in a harsh tone, "you too are a CEO."

When he is sure that he has caught Scott's full attention, he continues. "What do you think will happen to you, with your board, when they question you about impact on the bottom line, and you respond with gibberish about data flow and integration?"

Scott laughs nervously as he paints that picture in his mind. "My head would be handed to me on a silver platter," he admits.

"With or without an apple?" Craig inquires.

"Cut the jokes guys," Maggie interrupts impatiently. "Of course at the board level you can't use the language of system configurations and computer screen options. But that doesn't mean that better visibility is an empty phrase. Craig, why didn't you give them an example of better visibility. Something that they all can relate to and care about."

"Like?"

"Like the improvement in the time it takes to close your quarterly financial reports." Maggie replies. "One of the biggest problems of the chief financial officer, in every large company, and your company is not an exception, is to be able to report the actual financial results as close as possible to the end of the quarter.

"Since we completed the accounting module roll-out across

the company two quarters ago, you are already seeing improved financial information being available to all managers. The financial close cycle has been drastically improved. What used to take over forty-five days is now done in about ten days. Not to mention that the cost and effort required to prepare those reports is dramatically reduced."

"Good point," Scott confirms. "I know that my board would not like seeing the actual figures until a month and a half after the quarter is over."

Craig agrees. "You should have heard their comments when, for the first time in history, they got it only two weeks after the end of the quarter. They were delighted."

"So?" Maggie pushes on.

"So, of course I brought up this strong point. But the weasel just asked, 'what is the bottom line impact,' and all the chickens nodded."

"I see," says Scott. "Everybody wants the actual numbers as quickly as possible, but we don't know how to pin a dollar value onto getting these numbers earlier."

"That is exactly it," Craig says. "Most of the original justification is composed of such items, things that everybody will agree are nice to have. But when you ask what the real benefit is, in dollar terms, then they evaporate. Do you see my problem? I'm now stuck in a corner."

"But there is a bottom line impact." Maggie is far from giving up. "The cost to prepare those reports was dramatically reduced."

"Was it?" asks Craig.

"Of course it was." Maggie shuffles through her papers. "Take for example the cost to process a transaction line. According to your numbers, it was twelve point seven cents per line. Now, after installing the ERP system, it's only three point two cents. Here are real savings of almost ten cents for each line. Now multiply it by the number of transaction lines that have to be processed to prepare one quarter's financials. It must be mammoth savings. It's in the high millions."

Craig stops pacing and looks at her. He sighs. "These cents and fractions of cents that you are quoting, what are they based on?"

"On your numbers," Maggie answers.

"Yes, I know. But don't you see that they're based on the fact that our good ERP system enables our people to waste less time processing the transactions?"

"Correct. That's a savings you realize from using our ERP."

Craig shakes his head. "There is no real savings here. True, it takes less time to process each transaction, but it still requires the same amount of people."

"How come?"

"Because we didn't lay off any of those people. That's reality Maggie. There was no head count reduction in the financial department."

And then he adds bitterly, "These financial people are very good at demanding cost reductions everywhere, but when it comes to their own turf, they are even better at protecting their people. What money did we save? We still pay the same salaries."

When Maggie doesn't answer, he continues, "Don't confuse cost accounting terms like reduction in the cost of a transaction line, or item-cost, with real cost reduction. No head-count reduction means no real cost reduction, no impact on the bottom line."

Maggie feels her cheeks flush.

Scott tries to summarize. "Information flow is streamlined, and even the board is enjoying it. Still, you can't translate those improvements to bottom line impact. That's one aspect. The other point is that making overhead personnel jobs easier is great, but there is no bottom line impact if we still employ the same number of people."

"You hit the nail on the head," Craig agrees, and begins to pace again. "Talking about head-count reduction? What we are seeing is just the opposite. There are more technogeeks running around here than ever before. We now have temporary trailers in the parking lot to hold all the extra people. The weasel must have noticed it when he came in for a board meeting. That's probably why he brought up the issue in the first place."

Craig stops and looks at each of them. "Obviously this is not something that we could talk about over the phone, you needed to be here in person. I need your help in identifying where the bottom line results will come from. There must be something convincing that we can come up with." After a second he adds, "And I need it soon!"

Maggie hears Scott take a deep breath before beginning to answer. She is glad that he's going to step in. Maggie is very uncomfortable with this situation. She's faced unsatisfied clients before, but for other reasons. Usually a customer has a right to be concerned. She gets called in personally when her team is over-budget, or late, never when the project is on time and within budget. This implementation is going so well, but Craig still has a real problem. A big problem. And if Craig has a problem, they have it too.

Scott begins, "You and I both know that the trailers are for temporary people who will go away when the project is completed."

"I know that, and the board knows it," Craig replies. "But when the trumpets call for blood, and the cry 'bottom line' is in the air, any cheap shot is allowed."

"Was it as bad as that?" Scott is sympathetic.

"Basically, yes." Craig finally settles into his chair.

"Let's go back to the issue of better visibility," Scott says confidently. "I agree with Maggie that it does have an impact. Craig, don't tell me that having the financial report much sooner doesn't have an impact. It does." He raises his hand to prevent Craig from commenting. "I also agree with you that it's hard to quantify the impact. So my suggestion is to look at other aspects that are impacted by the presence of better visibility. Maybe there it will be easier to connect it to bottom line impact."

"Agreed," says Craig. After a second he asks, "Like what?"

"Like the fact that sales information coming from the dozens of regional warehouses is now streamlined to the production plants."

"That's an excellent example." Maggie can't stop herself from jumping in. "In the past, how much time did it take from the minute a regional warehouse sold a product until the plant which produces that product knew about it? First, all the regional warehouses were reporting their sales, on a weekly basis, to the main office of their continent. Then each main office would sum it all up and pass it to headquarters. Then the professionals at headquarters would analyze the data, and finally, they issued a revised production forecast to the various plants. If I'm not mistaken, the time that elapsed between a sale in a regional warehouse and when it translated to a production schedule in a plant was how long? Three weeks?"

"If we were lucky," Craig agrees.

"Now," Maggie continues, "already in three divisions, that information is available at the plants the same day of the sale."

"And the bottom line?" Craig doesn't lose sight of the target.

"Not so fast, bear with me," Scott continues in the the line. "Let's trace the impact according to what we know about the workings of your organization. Due to our system, the plants know each day how much every distribution center, anywhere in the world, has sold of each product. Having the data of what has been sold in the distribution centers three weeks earlier than they used to means that the plants know three weeks earlier what is demanded of them. Not only does it improve the forecast, now they can plan their production according to actual market consumption."

"That makes sense," Craig says, and Maggie nods in agreement.

"Now what can we speculate about the impact of improving the response time from the plants to the distribution centers? Cutting it by three whole weeks?"

Nobody answers.

"Come on you two." Scott is a little impatient. "You have

spent all your life in the industry. Don't tell me that all the pressure on me to supply systems that will improve forecast and reduce lead times is there for no reason. There must be an impact."

"Faster response from the plants means," Craig thinks aloud, "shipping more of the right stuff to the right places." His expression starts to brighten. "That means that there will be fewer incidences of a warehouse running out of a product. Scott, you're lucky. You don't sell commodity products. We do, so almost every time a distribution center doesn't have a product that there is demand for, we lose sales to the competition."

Craig confidently concludes, "Fewer shortages in the distribution warehouses mean more sales. And more sales is more money. Real bottom line impact!"

"That's not the only impact," Maggie adds. "Having information about the actual sales immediately at the plants also means that the plants are shipping less of the wrong stuff to the wrong places."

"Good point," Craig says. "And that means less unneeded inventory in the warehouses."

"And having less unneeded inventory in the warehouse," Maggie is on a roll, "also has an impact on the bottom line. A big impact. Craig, how much inventory does Pierco hold in their warehouses?"

"Over two billion dollars. And if you ask me, most of it is the wrong inventory in the wrong places. So if the ERP system reduces it by, let's say, only twenty percent, on that item alone I have the bottom line justification." He turns to the intercom and then stops. "Maggie, do you have any numbers to confirm that inventory did go down?"

Maggie looks through her papers. The others are silent.

After a while she says, "For the division that went live on 'order entry' six months ago, I see a reported reduction of eighteen million dollars. On the other two, that went live last quarter, less than a million."

"Less than a million is nothing," Craig says, waving his

hand. "It's background noise. But eighteen million is a good start. What about sales lift? Do you have numbers on that?"

"I don't think I have it with me. Besides, we don't have all the numbers yet. Remember, we're still in the early phases. Two of the divisions have just started, and three more aren't scheduled to go live on the order entry module for two months."

"I know, I know," Craig says impatiently. "But we can safely extrapolate from the results of the division that has been using the system for quite some time," Craig half states, half asks.

"I don't see any reason why not," is Maggie's answer. "I think we should look into this. I can get an assessment team on it right away."

She glances at Scott to ensure that he is with her on this. "We can give you a full report of the expected improvement areas, and the timing when the cost reductions can be expected."

"Will you concentrate on all bottom line impacts, not just cost reduction?" Craig asks.

"Of course. I can have it ready for you in thirty days. Will that do?"

Craig shakes his head, but starts to smile. "Actually, the day before yesterday would have been much better. As it stands, my next board meeting is a month from yesterday. I need a few days to review it before the meeting. Let's say by July seventeenth. Can you make it?"

Realizing that she's just landed a very nice follow-on opportunity, Maggie confidently smiles and says sweetly, "Of course. That won't be a problem at all. Shall I put this on a change order to the current contract, or would you like a new one?"

Neither Scott nor Maggie say anything until they are back on the main highway.

Maggie sighs heartily and says, "That went better than I expected."

Getting no response from Scott, who is just humming to himself, Maggie continues with growing enthusiasm, "We are in the best situation we can hope for. Here's a CEO of a very large company, and we're saving his butt. Once I give him the ammunition he needs, startling bottom line justification, he will owe us. Personally. What a reference!"

Determined, she adds, "This implementation will finish on time and on budget—even if my company has to eat the difference in cost from what it really takes to get it done. In the end we will have here a terrific reference, with the CEO himself willing to testify. Grand. How do you like it?"

Scott is still humming. It doesn't bother Maggie even though she knows it means he has heard little of what she just said. She has learned over the years of working together that when Scott hums, he is working on something. Something important. It's okay. When he's ready, he will talk.

No, that won't do. They will arrive at the airport in less than half an hour and she's not flying back with Scott. She has to catch a flight to LA.

"Let's hear it," she prods him.

"I was just thinking . . ." Scott begins, and stops.

"Yes?"

He looks out the window.

"Scott!" Maggie insists.

"I think that we were just handed the key piece of an important puzzle."

"Which is?"

"For a long time I've been wondering why the sales efforts required to sell to a mid-range company are almost as massive as the efforts required for a large company. Yet the chances of success are even smaller. It shouldn't be like that. In a smaller company there are fewer managers that have to agree, fewer management levels, fewer committees that have to decide. Still it takes about the same time to close a deal, anywhere from six to eighteen months."

"That's a fact," Maggie states.

"Yes, but why?"

"Do you have an answer?"

"I'm not sure." Looking at her at last, Scott says, "I'm still trying to digest today's events. Have you noticed that when Craig asked for justification, my first inclination was to respond in computer system terms. I instinctively started to think and speak in terms of configurations and data flows. To force me to speak his language, to address his concerns, he had to practically hit me on the head."

"That's a fair description," Maggie says, adding salt to his wounds.

"Listen, Maggie, this is important. Don't you see, if I'm making this mistake, my people, who are less familiar with a top management perspective, are surely doing it as well. We are talking our language, the computer systems' language, not the clients'. That's a violation of the most basic rule of prudent sales."

"This is the first time you've noticed it?" Maggie is surprised. "What do you think the main function of my people is? They are literally the translators between your system and the client. To know your computer system inside and out is important for us," Maggie states. "But no less important is knowing how to speak the client's language; cost reduction, productivity improvement, lead-time reduction—the whole jargon."

Scott thinks about it for a while. "No Maggie. It's true that your people speak differently than my people, but . . ."

"Carry on," she presses him.

"Now I realize that we are dealing here with three different languages. There's the system language of configurations, screens, and options, which is very different from the middle level management language of lead-time reduction and productivity improvements."

"Of course," Maggie says.

"But there is yet a third language; the bottom line, the top manager's language. And that is the most important. They are talking dollars, net profit, return on investments cash. Neither my people nor yours are talking that language." Then he adds, "Of course these three languages are interconnected, but what became so evident today is that the translation is not trivial. As a matter of fact, we, or at least I, am ignorant of most of the translations."

"My people talk bottom line," Maggie argues. "Is 'cost' not bottom line terminology?"

"Maggie," Scott says softly, "have you forgotten the lesson on the cost reduction of a transaction line?"

Maggie blushes a little as she reconstructs Craig's words, "Don't confuse reduction in the cost of a transaction line with real cost reduction." "You're right, Scott. I agree. System integrators don't talk and think in terms of bottom line impact. Now explain what you mean by translations."

Scott gives an example. "We know, more or less, the connection between our system and the ability to close the quarterly financial books earlier. But the translation from closing books earlier to bottom line impact, I don't know. And neither do you or Craig."

Maggie doesn't answer.

"Don't you agree with me?" Scott is surprised.

"I do. Of course I do," Maggie winces. "I was wondering why the fact that our people don't speak top management language might be more important to smaller companies. Maybe they're even more risk averse and conservative than the big guys since they can less afford to make a mistake?"

"That's what I was thinking about. I still haven't figured it out. But I'm getting closer."

After a minute of silence Maggie says, "You know Scott, doing the business case for Pierco will be more tricky than I thought. I'll have to supervise it myself."

"Yes," Scott agrees. "Your staff is accustomed to using the standard templates. That will not do here."

"That's all right," Maggie says. "I'm sure we're going to learn a lot from doing this work."

"For sure. Please keep me informed."

"United," the driver announces.

As she picks up her bag, Maggie says, "Scott, one more thing to think about. I wonder how much the fact that we don't concentrate on bottom line benefits has distorted our implementations?"

"What made you think of that?"

"Just think what would happen if we could achieve bottom line results early in the implementation. How much easier it would be to handle the project!"

To the closed door Scott whispers, "Thanks Maggie. That's an important point."

Twenty minutes later, boarding his flight, he adds, "And how much unnecessary complexity has crept into our ERP system?"

He hums throughout the entire flight.

Chapter 6

"Flight attendants, prepare for landing."

Maggie shuts down and powers off her computer at the announcement. Almost got the e-mail cleaned up, she congratulates herself. Those power plugs in the seats are a blessing and a curse. Now there is no rest for the road weary. Reminding herself that now she can dig into those proposals as soon as she gets to the office, without worrying about e-mail, she finishes packing up her computer.

The plane rolls to the gate and is rocked side to side by the jetway operator.

"I guess we're here!" Maggie quips to the gentleman sitting next to her.

She walks quickly off the plane to her waiting driver. "How's the traffic on four-o-five this afternoon, Steve? Think we can make it to the office in under an hour?"

Steve nods, and replies, "It looked good on the way in but you know how fast it can change. I put some mineral water in the back for you. No bubbles, right?"

"That's right. Thanks, I really appreciate that. The air on the plane was so dry," Maggie says as she slides into the car. She turns on her cell phone to see what voice mail has shown up while she was in the air. There is an urgent message from the main office. What could happen in just a few hours, she wonders as she dials the familiar number.

"Oh, that's great!" Maggie exclaims, listening to a message. "That is just great." The project sure needed that boost.

She dials again. "Patrick," she says, "what happened with Sheila? I thought she was happy here."

Patrick answers, "I think the travelling was getting to her. SBL consulting made her an offer that she said she couldn't refuse. Less money but she gets to work locally. She did give us two weeks notice though."

"Big deal," Maggie retorts quickly, then repeats more quietly, "big deal. The Dubro project is only six weeks from going live, and the project manager leaves now? Getting a new project manager up to speed will take more than two short weeks!"

Patrick responds, "I know, and we don't have any project managers on the bench right now to fill in. Dubro is a big project and we need someone of the right caliber to head it. The problem is that anyone who might be appropriate is already heading a project that is no less important."

"Are you sure?"

"Maggie, I went over it very carefully, and I'm telling you, that in my opinion, we don't have anyone of the right caliber who we can afford to pull off their current assignment. Just in case, I put in a call to Lela to see if any of new hires will work."

"With only six weeks from go-live, we are not going to assign a new hire," Maggie snaps.

"I know. So it looks like there's no choice but to pull a good person from another project."

Maggie reserves decisions such as these for herself. It is a delicate matter. One of the prime considerations is to minimize the amount of damage to whatever project that person gets pulled from. There's no point in trading one potential fiasco for another.

"For starters, get me a status on the D&K project," she says. "If I remember right, they're in playback stage, so we can spring Mark for Dubro, and what's his name can cover at D&K for a while."

At the same time, a nagging feeling hits Maggie in the gut. She suspects that Sheila would not be leaving if everything was going well at Dubro. Through the years, she has learned to listen to that intuition.

In a softer tone she continues, "Also, please send me, to our LA office, a copy of the last Dubro steering committee report, and the internal audit file. I want to see exactly where we are."

"You got it," Patrick answers. "Anything else?"

"Not right now," Maggie responds.

"Doing the project manager shuffle like I have nothing better to think about," she mutters to herself. Still, she learned early on that being directly involved with project manager assignments is of key importance to her operation. The right project manager means early warning about potential problems. Early warning means early resolution, and early resolution means happy customers. Happy customers mean good references, and good references mean more business. That's what it all boils down to, she reminds herself.

Since the early days, supervising the implementation jobs has been the hard part. KPI has grown by leaps and bounds in six short years. And so it should! KPI Solutions delivers successful projects. Maggie has made her reputation in the implementation business by using only experienced people. No kids straight out of college for her company—no sir! Experience has taught her that—the hard way.

The college kids are cheap, and some of them are bright. They make your hourly rate look great in the bid, but the customers get really upset when they realize the incredible price they are paying for someone with no experience. Successful real-world experience is worth paying for, but damn hard to find. Supervising the projects and the search for people to do the projects—these are the constants in her life these days.

She dials again. "Good morning, Lela. How is everything there? Did you finish the preliminary interviews for that last batch of resumés that came over the Internet?"

It wasn't so long ago that Maggie herself did the last interview for every person that joined her company. It is her reputation, after all, that each employee must work to maintain. At this point, it is simply too much. Still, she does her best to personally interview anyone who is destined for a project-manager slot. "How many got through Bill for me to talk to?" she asks.

"He wants what!" Maggie exclaims after Lela informs her of a requested starting salary. "And a signing bonus, too? One thing for sure, he has the nerve we're looking for." Then she adds, "If he turns out to be half as good as he says he is, he'll be worth it! Confirm his background, and if he checks out, put him on my calendar for an appointment in thirty minutes."

The salaries for these people have grown fast—even faster than KPI's phenomenal growth. Maggie smiles. KPI has grown even bigger than BGSoft—as measured in people anyway, she reminds herself. It would be fun to pass Scott in revenues, too. Who says the student can't outgrow the teacher? she chuckles to herself.

Still, salaries are not the most important things to these people. The money is more than just money. The salaries are the recognition, the validation, the confirmation of their success. That is what's important to these folks. Her people thrive on the challenge and thrill of overcoming each obstacle that stands in their way.

That kind of internal drive is not something you can teach. You either have it or you don't, and those that have it are rare indeed. When I see it, I hire the person, even if there isn't a project for them immediately. Keeps me one step ahead of the competition. They don't have the balls to take that risk. They try to staff up after winning a project, and fall flat on their face.

Be paranoid. Scott has taught her well. Don't ever assume that the best price or best proposal will win. People who assume can still lose. Make sure the deck is stacked in your favor, and then keep pushing.

The competition has a hard time keeping their footing when Maggie's Marines go on a mission. Customers just love meeting the project team that will work with them even before they sign. Creating the right chemistry from the beginning makes for a successful sale and a successful implementation. Planting that seed early in the sell cycle grows into a key point when the final decision is made. And just call me the happy harvester, she giggles to herself.

Just then her cell phone rings. "Good afternoon, this is Maggie," she says brightly.

"Sorry to bother you again, but Mr. Cane just called and he refused to talk to me. He insists on talking to you directly," Patrick explains.

"Did Bob say what it's about?" Maggie asks.

"He really didn't say. But as I already warned you, there are some problems there. I will send the full report to your office."

"Why can't they call me when they're happy? Fine, I'll call him as soon as I have reviewed your report."

Knowing Bob Cane, this call will not be as pleasant as seeing Craig this morning had been. So much for getting on those proposals right away. She sighs, and thinks about the duck picture on the wall of her personal office. Scott gave it to her as a reminder of how to get through situations just like these. Stay calm on the surface, but paddle like crazy underneath.

Maggie hardly slows her stride as she moves through the front lobby. She calls out to Dorothy, the LA office manager. "Did you get some reports from Patrick for me? Please bring them into my office. Also, please run the latest staffing assignments and bring those too."

Before her laptop has had time to boot up, Dorothy is at the door. "Here are the reports you asked for."

"Will everybody arrive for our four o'clock briefing?"

"Everyone was notified, and they're already here, except for Larry of course."

"What about Larry?"

Dorothy hesitates. "He said that you approved his absence."

"Yes, I did," Maggie recalls. Larry has to give his briefing to his client's steering committee. It will require a real tap dance on his part since the project is almost a year behind schedule. Everything that can go wrong, did, and then some. Poor Larry. But he's good. He will pull it through.

"Do you need anything else?" Dorothy inquires.

"Not right now," Maggie replies. All the reports she asked for are here already. Patrick is up to his normal efficiency. Turning first to Bob Cane's report, she begins to read. In a few minutes, she hits the button on the intercom.

"Dorothy, get Patrick on the phone. Tell him I want more details on the delayed software changes that he says are holding up the Cane project."

Before she calls Bob back, she needs to fully understand both sides of the story. Why can't anyone ever really implement the 'vanilla' version like they say they will at the beginning of the project, she wonders.

Trying to figure out how much leeway to add into the schedule to cover for things like this is a real art. She is sure that Bob is calling her to complain about when this project will really finish, and how much it will really cost. According to the initial schedule, it was supposed to be complete four months ago. Of course, he conveniently forgets that he demanded that all the software changes be done before they went live, rather than listening to the project manager's advice.

Learn how to do business with the new system first, and only then can you ask for changes. That is Maggie's first law of implementation. And she's sure her people conveyed this to Bob.

Too much money is wasted on changes that make the new software look like the previous version. When will they realize that if the new system looks exactly like the old system, then change is unnecessary? Shaking her head, Maggie reminds herself of rule two: the customers are not always right, but they are always the customers.

It looks like she will be talking to Lenny again soon. Why can't they just get this stuff done when they promise it? She shakes her head. It's five minutes to four, time to head to the conference room.

Two hours later she returns to her office. Thank God, no new crises were revealed. As a matter of fact, the LA team is doing quite well. All things considered, of course. She looks at the two pages of notes she scribbled during the meeting. Nothing is urgent, except for . . . She circles three items, and picks up the phone.

Too late, she realizes, it's way after office hours on the East Coast. She pages Dorothy again on the intercom.

"Dorothy, before you leave, could you order me some dinner from that little Italian place I like?"

After Dorothy expresses her parental concern, Maggie replies in a cold tone, "I appreciate your concern, but I want to get these proposals done before I leave for Dallas tomorrow morning. Just get me some pasta primavera and a salad. Thanks.

"Just what I need—another mother," Maggie mutters.

While marking the proposals, Maggie starts to think about the meeting with Craig this morning. With a sigh, she realizes that she still needs to assign a team to that project, too. With all the fuss this afternoon, it just slipped her mind. She will also have to find the time to coach this team. Scott is right, if the team uses the standard templates there is no way that they will satisfy Craig's needs. She shudders to think what would happen if Craig doesn't have enough to take to his board.

Back to work, she chides herself. Have to get these proposals finished so that Gail's people can get the deals closed.

"One guy by the tie." The customers sure like that saying. "One guy by the tie." No finger pointing between the software company and the implementation team allowed—those are the new rules of the game. Providing one integrated proposal to the customer reduces the fear factor inherent in a project like this, and helps finish business.

But, Maggie wonders, where does Craig's bottom-line discussion come in here? Will all clients start to demand real bottom line justifications? Does this mean the rules are changing again?

Back to work, she tells herself sharply. If I don't take care of the present, I won't have a future to worry about.

Chapter 7

JULY 5, 1998

We're just a head of animals stampeding toward the cliff, Scott thinks, twisting nervously in his bed. Actually it's even worse. The ERP vendors have to constantly increase their speed. Forty percent a year to be exact.

And no one is blinking an eye; everybody in the industry behaves as if the cliff does not exist. Troubled, he turns over again.

Can it be that they simply don't see where we're all heading? It can't be. By now it's not just a logical prediction, it has become a painful reality that we're all forced to struggle with. He groans. "They don't talk for the same reason I don't talk."

A protest comes from the other side of the bed.

Quietly, Scott gropes his way out of the bedroom. When he reaches the stairs, he switches on the lights. And I don't talk because sounding the alarm will not help and could hurt. It definitely could hurt.

He reaches the kitchen and pours himself a big glass of milk. His mind keeps on racing. It's the first time he has faced a situation that looks hopeless. The walls are closing in on them and there's nothing he can do to prevent it. Their main market is saturated and he can't do a thing about the fact that there are a limited number of large companies.

He sits down, holding the full glass between his hands. Gail is wrong. There are not that many companies who are so dissatisfied with their ERP system that they will consider writing off their huge investment and starting all over again with a new vendor. There are a few, enough to meet this quarter's number and maybe the next one, but what then? What then?

We'll have to concentrate on the mid-market. That's the obvious direction. But the more he looks at it, the more he realizes that it doesn't provide a real solution. With the long and expensive sales cycle, and the abysmal revenues they get from a mid-range client, there are not enough margins to support their current operation. Let alone to support the required growth rate.

Not having a market is one heck of a problem. But now there is another problem on top of it. According to Lenny, it wouldn't be long before we don't have a product, either.

Lenny returned from India two days ago. His way of facing major difficulties is to joke about them. No wonder Scott was not delighted when Lenny started his update with, "What do you want to hear first, the good news or the bad news?"

Scott picks up the still full glass, turns on the lights above the garden and heads outside. He starts aimlessly pacing the large garden. The good news is that version eight is ready. The bad news is that the high expectations that Lenny had will not materialize.

That doesn't include the impact of version eight on sales. That front looks like it exceeds Gail's expectations. Her people were able to use the announcement of the simple architecture to bring in more sales, enough to finish the quarter on the nose. And the prospect of winning over some of the competitors' clients is very promising. So promising that Gail, for the first time this year, is not concerned about the rest of the year.

But the bad news makes all that meaningless. Lenny is now convinced that the new architecture will have little, if any impact on the ease of servicing the system. It will not be easier to add new features, it will not shrink the time to bring new people up to speed, and most importantly, it will not be easier to locate or fix bugs.

"Scott, in six months we'll look back with nostalgia on the time we could supply a fix in less than two weeks," were Lenny's words. "Our entire support system is rapidly heading toward a total collapse, and I don't know what to do."

They have exhausted the market, and the product has become too complex to handle. But the real problem is that they don't know what to do about it.

Scott, careful not to spill the milk, lowers himself into a lounge chair near the swimming pool. Not knowing what to do, his mind drifts.

Things were just the opposite when they started. Now they have a bright present and a dark future. Way back then, they had almost no present, but they were shooting for a glorious future. They knew exactly what should be done. They had a clear vision and they had a good strategy. They even had reasonable tactics.

Not that it was easy. Not at all. They didn't have the recognition, they didn't have enough money, they were constantly oscillating between not having enough clients and not having enough people. In retrospect, what they were actually lacking was the experience needed to grow a company. But they had the one thing that compensated for everything else, that they knew where they were headed. Not any more.

Scott puts the glass of milk on the ground. He feels even more troubled than before. He is too young to live in the past. Besides, that would be admitting defeat, and Scott, being the warrior that he is, won't stand for it.

He jumps up. There must be a way! Pacing the garden paths again, he forces himself to reexamine the BGSoft situation. He must find a crack in the closing walls.

As it stands, they still have about six months until the avalanche starts, until they'll be on the way to missing the forecast. Right now they can gain more time. Outside the US and Europe there are still many large companies that haven't yet bought an ERP system. Directing more efforts to South America, for example, will give them more breathing space.

But that's not a solution. That's only buying some more time. Be paranoid, he reminds himself. It helps, because he now realizes that he actually has less time than he thought.

The reality is that the ERP industry is reaching the edge of the cake. That is the reason that his short-term strategy is now based on grabbing a bigger piece of that limited cake, swaying competitors' clients to work with BGSoft. But that means that if BGSoft is successful, as he expects it to be, some competitors will not make their growth-rate targets. As a matter of fact, one or two will soon have to report negative growth. Nothing bad about that, except for the fact that it will definitely wake up Wall Street. The analysts will no doubt come to him and demand solid proof that the same fate is not awaiting BGSoft. And then, if he doesn't provide something convincing, his shares will nose-dive too.

So what's the way out? What can he do that will drastically shrink the sell cycle to the mid-market? Or alternatively, what can he do that will drastically simplify their software?

No. Solving just one of these problems without solving the other will not prevent the tumble of BGSoft. They must solve them both. Having a simple-to-service system with nobody to sell it to will not help. Likewise, being able to sell the system without being able to deliver it properly, once again, will not help.

From his experience Scott had learned that even if a problem looks insurmountable there is a simple and powerful solution. But such a solution can be found only if the scope is enlarged; only if the problem is viewed within the scope of a bigger picture.

Here he has two problems for which they don't have solutions, so it is reasonable to expect that the larger picture he has to look at is the one that contains them both.

If he wants to find a powerful, yet simple, solution he must also look at the connections between these problems.

Scott forces himself to go over the situation systematically. Lenny verbalized the problem they have with the product very succinctly. To satisfy the market demand, they must continue to add more and more features, which means they must continue to complicate the system. But in order to give adequate service, they must simplify the system. The dilemma they have with the product is clear, but this dilemma is the same whether targeting the large-size or the mid-size market.

At the same time, the problem of the market is evident. To maintain reasonable margins they have to sell mainly to large companies. But since there are not enough large companies left, to maintain the sales volume, they have to sell mainly to the mid-sized companies. The dilemma they have with the market is clear, but this dilemma is the same whether they continue to complicate the product or not.

The two dilemmas do not look connected. If it weren't for the self-discipline he had developed over the years, he would have shouted out of sheer frustration. Instead, he continues walking, kicking the pebbles that line the trail.

There must be something that I don't understand, he concludes. And if I don't fully understand the problems, how can I hope to find a solution?

Another pebble is kicked into the bushes.

In his attempt to find a starting point Scott asks himself if there is something specific that he doesn't understand regarding any one of these two problems.

There is such a thing. There is something that has puzzled him for a long time and is strongly connected to one of the dilemmas.

The reason for having abysmal margins in selling to the mid-range market is because the sales cycle is so long. But why is it that the sell cycle for mid-sized companies is as long as the sell cycle for large companies? And the chances of closing a deal are lower? It doesn't make any sense.

He finds himself back at the swimming pool. He sits down and picks up the milk. The glass is still full, but he empties it in less than ten seconds.

When was the last time he struggled with that mystery? It was after the lesson he got from Craig, when he realized that the entire ERP industry is not aimed toward bottom-line value. Not the software providers, not the system integrators, not even the client's IT people.

After that meeting, his intuition told him that confining their thinking to the language of computer systems, or even to the language of operations, is the problem. That might be the reason for the difficulties they face in the mid-market. The key must lie in the fact that they are not concentrating on bringing bottom-line value.

At that time, Maggie's prudent remarks had guided him, and directed his thinking to the impact it has on unnecessarily complicating the product. Neglecting to consider the bottom line has a major impact on the number of meaningless features that clients are constantly demanding. That drastically increases the system's complexity. But how exactly is it tied to the long sales cycle they experience in the mid-market?

If he can answer that question, he will establish a strong connection between the two dilemmas. Then he will probably be able to consider the product and the market simultaneously.

Scott is still walking and kicking pebbles when the sun comes up.

Chapter 8

She looks up from her notes and sees George sitting down at the end of the table. Maggie hadn't even noticed him enter the room. She smiles. "Good afternoon." Glancing at her watch she adds, "Where is Gail? She was supposed to be here at three."

"I heard there was an accident on the crosstown expressway."

"Did your team finish with Pierco's bottom-line justification?" Maggie asks George.

We finished what we could do. Which is not much. Most of the time was spent debating what can be considered a measurable benefit. The only thing that we agree on is that it knocked out many of the items we usually use in a system justification, like integration and visibility."

"Measurable benefit is not good enough for Craig," Maggie comments. "You can measure the reduction in number of defective parts, or in the time it takes now to process a transaction, but that doesn't yet give Craig his bottom line justification."

"Right, bottom-line impact. I know."

Just then Gail enters the conference room. "Good afternoon. How is everything here in paradise?"

Maggie smiles, "Paradise? You always had a great sense of humor, Gail. How was the trip over? Was the traffic terrible? Pretty soon we'll need a helicopter to get between offices in a reasonable time."

"Yeah. I'm exhausted. Do you have any tea?"

Maggie smiles. "Of course, right over there. I think there are a few different brands."

While Gail fixes her tea, Maggie's thoughts turn to the rest of her busy day. Two more meetings, and then a dinner with a customer. George had better have made real progress.

As she sits down, Gail says, "So it looks like we're going to win over Tesko as well. I hope you have enough people to put on the job."

"Don't worry, things are under control. You just keep on bringing them in."

"Good afternoon, Gail." George speaks up. "Maggie, the projector is working and ready if you want to get started. We haven't made this pretty yet, but I think that all the data are here."

George begins with a history of the Pierco's project, and the top-level rollout plan. Maggie impatiently interrupts him.

"We already know this part. Remember—we were there. On time and on budget. Blah blah blah. Craig wants the bottom line results for his board, not a history lesson."

George smiles. He knows that Maggie isn't upset with him personally. She has a way of cutting to the core of any issue. Her way of doing this intimidates some people, but George has grown accustomed to it. He quickly clicks through a couple more slides. On the screen appears the title: "Expected benefits for Pierco."

"Is this what you're looking for?"

Gail opens her laptop and prepares herself to take copious notes.

George begins to discuss the first point. "They can expect improved information for better management decisions." Maggie makes a face. That does not deter George from continuing "The project has developed and implemented master data standards for account numbers, parts, and vendors. This standardized data will allow an integrated corporate view, and provide the base for immediate profitability analyses for all product lines."

"Come on George, we talked about this," Maggie reacts. "How will that drive to the bottom line? Does it decrease cost or increase revenue?"

George fidgets in his chair and responds, "Well, this is a strategic benefit for the company rather than something quantifiably economic. I told the team that this wasn't going to fly, but they felt very strongly about it and its importance to Pierco."

Gail, while typing furiously, nods in agreement.

Maggie is less impressed. "It is important, but right now we need to show economic bottom-line benefits. What have you got with dollar signs and numbers," she urges him.

"Okay, okay. How about this? Because many of their invoices contained mistakes, the customers had to send a debit back. Using our ERP, customer debits will be reduced. Last year this figure totalled eight-hundred-million dollars."

Maggie leans forward. "You mean the system implementation will increase their revenue by eight-hundred-million? That makes the business case right there." Her voice is dripping with sarcasm.

Shaking his head, George responds, "No, they didn't miss the revenue, they just resent corrected invoices to their customers."

"Then how can this be claimed as a bottom-line benefit?" Maggie asks dryly.

Gail looks a little confused but she starts to smile.

George explains. "It takes time and significant manual effort at Pierco to get it fixed. Collection on the receivable by Pierco is significantly delayed."

Gail hesitantly asks, "So how does that come through on the bottom line?"

George continues, "The integration of BGSoft means that the invoice should be correct the first time. Pierco should get their money more quickly from their customers since the invoice is correct. And that means improved cash flow."

Maggie shakes her head again. "Good. But what number reaches the bottom line? That's what we want on the slide, George."

"Easier said than done," George replies. "You can't believe how much time was spent trying to convert the reduction in customer debits, from eight hundred million dollars to almost zero, into a bottom line number. Until we realized that we simply had to forget about that."

"What?" Maggie is not happy. "There is a bottom line benefit here. What do you mean you had to forget about it?"

"Maggie, give us some credit," George tries to calm her down. "What I mean is that we had to forget about the eight hundred million dollars and instead to concentrate on the final impact, on the resulting reduction in the amount of time that the receivables are still not collected. Then, of course, we wasted more effort trying to estimate what the total reduction would be."

"I don't understand," Maggie comments.

"In retrospect, neither do I," George smiles. "But you see, we're only used to doing this type of business justification before a project is approved. We were never before asked to do it after the project was well under way. So I'm not surprised it took us quite a while to adjust.

"In a way, it's easier. We don't have to make so many speculations since we finished the financial rollout eight months ago. The first division has been live for almost a year. We now have solid numbers."

"What has the actual reduction been in the average number of days Pierco has to wait until it gets the money?" Maggie asks.

George brings up the next slide. "Down by almost three days."

"That's all?" Gail is surprised.

"Don't sneeze at it. For a company the size of Pierco, one that sells close to ten billion dollars a year, this small cut in the number of days they wait until they actually collect represents a lot of money." And George brings up the next slide.

"Based on the results achieved to-date, we estimate that the onetime increase in cash will be close to eighty million dollars. And considering the interest rates that Pierco is paying, it means that the increase in profits is almost seven million dollars."

"Only seven million," Maggie says, clearly disappointed.

"Yes, that's all."

"What about the cost savings in handling the mistaken invoices?" Gail asks.

"It amounts to zero," George says in a flat tone. Noticing Gail's surprised expression, he explains. "To enable a smooth implementation of the ERP system, Pierco promised its employees that no one would be laid off as a result of having the new system."

"No reduction in head count, no cost saved," Maggie snaps. "That last realization sure pulls the carpet out from under a lot of our standard justifications, and seven million dollars to profits is not even a good start. George, what else do you have?"

George turns back to his computer and brings up the next item. "The new system means that Pierco did not have to do Y2K mitigation on eighty-seven legacy systems. The vendor cost alone was quoted at ninety-five-million and did not include Pierco's time. We should be able to claim that as a direct benefit."

Maggie nods her head. "Yes, we can use that to help justify the system purchase. But it is not an ongoing bottom-line impact. It's like you telling your wife how much money you saved her when you bought that new power saw last week. Yes, it was on sale. However, did your savings account go up after you bought it?"

George chuckles, "My wife said the same thing. Still, it was a good deal . . ."

With humor in her voice, Maggie continues, "Come on George, we must have more than this. How about material-cost reduction?"

"Well, material cost isn't even on the list. We looked at it, but the numbers just seemed too small to bother."

Maggie can see George getting frustrated. She encourages him by saying, "Pierco is such a large company that even a small decrease in material costs would go a long way. Surely they have seen some early results with the consolidation of purchasing in the first two divisions? It's only logical to expect that when purchasing is not done by each plant separately, the quantities are larger, and they can squeeze lower prices from the vendors."

"What can I say?" George shrugs. "The first division went live on the purchasing module nine months ago, and is reporting savings of seventy-eight-thousand dollars. Big deal." And he moves to bring the next item.

"Wait," Maggie stops him. "Each plant in that division uses totally different chemicals. So consolidating the purchasing for that division should amount to squat. What about the second division, the one that went live five months ago? All their plants use basically the same materials."

"We haven't checked." George is apparently embarrassed. "Give me a minute. He begins to look at the pile of financial papers he brought with him. His face brightens. "Yes, that division is reporting a material-cost reduction of six million annually."

Maggie smiles.

George is quick to recover. "Knowing the nature of the other divisions, my educated guess is that it will boil down to something around thirty million dollars in savings for the whole corporation. Of course, to firmly establish this number, we'll have to look into the details."

"Nice," Maggie beams. "And that's a result we can claim as

an ongoing, annual benefit. Without the change in the system, the material costs would have been higher next year, too.

"So now our system is justified on a eight year return-on-investment. Not good enough . . ."

Gail steps in and tries to help. "What about inventory impact? At least that would trade one asset investment for another—inventory for technology."

"Yes, that's the next item," George says brightly. "The first division to go live on the order-entry module, almost seven months ago, has already seen an eighteen million dollar inventory reduction. The other divisions have seen less than a million so far, but they've just started. Using the first division as a reference, we can project that the impact next year will be an inventory reduction of up to one-hundred-and-fifty-million, throughout the corporation."

Maggie encourages him, "And how will that show up on the bottom line?"

George responds, "The reduction in inventory will free up cash."

"Absolutely George. That is the effect on the balance sheet," Maggie says happily. "And what happens when that hits the Profit and Loss Statement?"

"The P&L will be affected by the fact that the cost of carrying that inventory is reduced," George quickly responds.

"What are you using as the inventory-carrying cost?" Gail inquires.

"I'm still waiting to get that number from them. Should we assume ten percent?"

"No, no," Maggie says. "Ten percent is just the cost of capital. They also consider the risk of obsolescence and damage, and the cost of the warehouses. I bet they use at least thirty percent for carrying cost."

George looks very happy. "Thirty percent of one-hundred-and-fifty-million is . . ." He punches the keys on his calculator.

"Forty-five million," Maggie helps him.

"That's right." Raising his eyes from his calculator, George agrees. "Now we have something."

"In a flat tone, Maggie comments," Not enough. Considering the havoc implementing our system caused in every corner of Pierco, a four-year justification is not enough for Craig to defend himself. We need more."

George puts his head on his hand and asks "So, where do we look next? I've exhausted my list. What's left are only things that we weren't able to convert to bottom-line numbers."

Maggie recalls the conversation she and Scott had with Craig and asks, "The inventory reductions that you've identified, where did they happen?"

"What do you mean?"

"In the plants or in the distribution centers?"

"I don't know." He flips through his papers. After a short while he gives the answer. "In distribution. Why is that important?"

"The reason for the inventory reduction is that our system cut almost three weeks from the replenishment cycle. That must have a parallel impact in distribution. There should be less stock outs as well."

"Yes. On that we have hard numbers." George is pleased. "Just a minute, I'll find them. Here it is. Their delivery performance improved from eighty-six to ninety-one percent. Maggie, the team had identified fewer stock outs as a benefit, but that doesn't directly tie in to a bottom-line impact."

Gail jumps in. "Fewer stock outs? Doesn't that usually mean higher sales, since the customer wouldn't have to buy a competitor's product?"

"That's what we thought too," George says. "But when we looked at the numbers, the revenues were basically flat."

Maggie is disappointed. "So we'll have to go with what we have."

"Wait a minute," Gail persists. "Improved due-date performance will usually not cause a huge jump in sales, but we should expect a one or two percent increase. Such small increases can easily be hidden in the fluctuation of sales from one month to the next. George, you say that you have data for six months?"

"Yes."

"If the sales of this division are stable, on the huge volume that Pierco is selling, maybe we can detect a one percent increase," Maggie joins in. "Where is the data? Do you have it as a graph?"

They examine the graph. There is a slight increase. Using a ruler, they determine the slope. "We can safely state that there is an increase of at least two-and-a-half percent," George finally concludes.

"George, let's play it on the conservative side and include only a two percent sales lift for the other divisions," Maggie instructs. "What will the impact be?"

"Two percent lift in sales, for Pierco, means an additional two-hundred-million dollars a year. And we know," George says confidently, "that their average product margins are twenty-seven percent."

"Hefty margins," Gail comments.

"You have to remember that they're vertically integrated," George explains, then continues, "that means that the additional net profit a year, once the system rolls out to all divisions, will be about . . . fifty million dollars a year. Maggie, we have what you wanted. The justification is even better than what we had when we started the project."

"So it seems." Maggie is relieved. "But let's go over it. The onetime savings are coming mainly from the reduction in outstanding receivables, the Y2K and the inventory reductions. Between the three, we have how much? About three-hundred-million. Since they paid only three-hundred-and-twenty for the software and the implementation, it means that Pierco is actually getting the system for free.

"But not less important are the ongoing benefits. Again, those stem from the inventory reduction, the consolidation in purchasing, and the lift in sales, and they amount to over one-hundred-and-twenty-million dollars a year. Craig is going to emerge from this smelling like a rose. That's beautiful."

"Let me finish the rest of this," George says, full of vigor, "and I'll have it to you by the day after tomorrow."

"Terrific. Excellent job, George. Excellent." She glances at her watch. "And we finished early. Gail, thanks for taking the time to sit in on this."

"Scott suggested it. He said it would be an eye-opener, and he was right," Gail replies.

"Yes," George agrees. "For me it was quite a shock."

As they exit, he adds, "So many of the standard benefits we list in our system justification are really small, or aren't benefits at all when we consider the bottom line. I think that from our standard list of twenty points, only three have made it. And can you imagine, an increase in sales, which turns out to be so important, wasn't on our list at all!"

Chapter 9

Before going to bed, Gail does a last check of her e-mail. One message immediately catches her eye. It's from Scott, and the subject reads. "Not urgent but important."

"Interesting," she whispers to herself as she opens it. Like every e-mail from Scott, it is very short. "Thank you for your clear notes. When can you meet me? Ask Lenny to join in."

What notes? Gail wonders. Oh, it must be my notes from the meeting with Maggie and George. While bringing up her itinerary, she wonders what could be so important about those notes. Her schedule is jampacked for the rest of the week, and everything looks important.

"Not urgent," wrote Scott, "but important." Her curiosity grows. It can't be the notes themselves, it must be some insight that Scott hopes to gain from them. Did he discover something that can help maintain our growth rate? She can't imagine such a miracle, but with Scott, anything is possible. Well, there's only one way to find out.

After talking with Lenny on the phone, she writes an e-mail to

81

Scott suggesting a meeting at nine A.M. For the next ten minutes she is busy writing e-mails, clearing the entire morning.

"Lenny, did you have a chance to go over Gail's notes?" Scott asks.

"Yes, nothing new."

Gail is surprised. What does he mean by 'nothing new'? "Isn't it new to you that the way we usually justify our system has so little to do with the bottom line?"

"Yesterday's news, Gail." Lenny is grinning. "Scott told me all about it when he returned from his visit to Pierco. Your notes just confirm it."

Show off, she thinks.

Turning to Scott, Lenny continues. "As I already told you, it does not have any effect on our system. Take, for example, the new features that I've just now authorized. In my opinion, none of them will contribute even one cent to any client's bottom line. But it doesn't matter. The clients demand it, and we have to respond to the clients' demands. That's life," he finishes with a sigh.

Gail thinks about it, then says, "I agree."

"Well, I don't agree," says Scott.

Lenny can usually read Scott's mind pretty well. Not this time. When Lenny is embarrassed, he usually jokes. "Gail, you get what Scott is saying? He just said that we don't have to respond to the clients' demands. That's news! Problem solved! No more stupid features."

She doesn't bother smiling.

"I don't agree that the information in Gail's notes doesn't have ramifications on our system." Scott leans back in his armchair and declares, "As a matter of fact, I think that what we got yesterday has major ramifications not just on our system, but on every aspect of how we do business."

Lenny's face lights up. "Wow, so you solved the problem. Not a minute too early. Let's hear it."

"What we got yesterday," Scott starts to explain, "is the true value of our system for a large company. I say the true value, because it is the first time I've seen a justification stripped of all the brou-ha-ha of admiration of technology. It isn't cluttered with vague words like 'visibility' or 'productivity,' or even 'dead-time.' It's just the hard dollar benefits.

"Yesterday evening, I did a simple, logical exercise. I took Pierco's justification, and I tried to see what the benefits would have been if Pierco was worth a hundred million dollars, rather than ten billion. The results are quite surprising. Shall we go over it together?"

They both nod, not out of politeness, but because they are genuinely interested.

"The benefits to Pierco are due to five main items," Scott says, starting to do the analysis. "The five items are: reduction in days of outstanding receivables, Y2K . . ."

"Scott," Gail interrupts, "let's ignore the impact of Y2K. Every company that's concerned about it has already decided on the actions to take. I think that Y2K is no longer a factor in any company's decision to upgrade its computer systems."

"I agree," says Lenny.

Scott starts again. "So, the benefits are coming from four items; reduction in days of outstanding receivables, reduction in material costs, reduction in inventory, and increase in sales. The analysis KPI did for Pierco gives us vital information. It gives us the reasons for these improvements.

"The reason for the reduction in outstanding days is the fact that our system enables the client to generate invoices with fewer mistakes. On this item, do you see any difference between a large company and a small one?"

After a moment Lenny answers, "Not really. A smaller company also generates invoices with mistakes. Of course, a smaller company won't gain as many millions from having the invoices right the first time, but a smaller company doesn't have to pay so much for our system. I don't see any reason to believe that the relative impact from this item is much different for a smaller company."

Scott looks at Gail, who says, "I agree, but this item isn't that important. It gives just a onetime contribution to cash, and the impact on profit is negligible. Let's move on."

Scott does. "The reduction in material costs is due to consolidating the purchasing for all plants in the company. Do you see any difference here?"

"A big difference," Gail is quick to answer. "A smaller company might have only one or two plants. In that case consolidation of purchasing will amount to nothing, or close to it."

"That's interesting," Lenny observes. "On this item, the less geographically diverse the company, the less value it gets. Even in relative terms. And of course, smaller companies tend to be much less diverse than large companies."

"Correct," Scott confirms. "Now let's move to the last two items on our list, the inventory reduction, and the sales increase. Both are the result of the same change, the reduction in the time the information takes to get from the many regional distribution centers to the production plants."

"Same thing," Gail is quick to notice. "A smaller company might not have a distribution network at all. And if it has, it is definitely much smaller than Pierco's worldwide distribution network. The less diverse the company's operations, the fewer benefits they are going to get. Hell, for most smaller companies, these last two items will amount to practically zero!"

"Scott, I see where you are heading," Lenny remarks. "But before you reach a conclusion, let me make one remark. There's one big item that we don't see in Pierco's case. The savings due to reduction in manpower."

Before Scott has a chance to answer, Gail interjects. "Pierco is not an exception. In most companies, in order to reduce the resistance to change, they give some type of promise that nobody, or almost nobody, will get hurt because of the new technology."

"Still the potential here is big." Lenny is not fully convinced.

"Lenny, I'm out there every day," Gail says impatiently "and I'm telling you that savings from layoffs are relatively small. So far I haven't seen even one case where substantial layoffs were done as a result of implementing our system. Scott, I think that we can take the Pierco case as quite representative."

"I agree," says Scott. "It might be that KPI, when they did the analysis for Pierco, neglected to consider some additional benefits. It might be that for other companies there are some additional benefits. But the conclusion is the same: the smaller the company, the less it stands to gain from our technology. Even in relative terms."

Lenny is willing to accept that. "So what you're telling us is that for the large companies, we offer a tremendous bargain, but for the mid-range companies, we're offering very little real value?!"

"I tend to agree." Gail is thoughtful. "I've always claimed that mid-sized companies are not a good market for us."

"Why?" Lenny asks.

"Isn't it obvious?" Gail answers. "If we don't bring enough real value, only the people who admire new technology, who think that they must be modern, must move with the current fashion, only they will buy our system."

Immediately she adds, "Thank God there are lots of them. But of course, not everybody in a company is a technology freak, so if we don't offer real value it takes much more time and effort to overcome the resistance of the skeptics."

"Gail, give me some credit," Lenny says. "I understand all that. What I mean is that we can do something about it."

"What?" And without letting Lenny answer, she continues. "We have tried to tailor a mini-system for the mid-market. Did it help? No. For any feature that we trim there are always some mid-size companies that need it. Now we see that even if we had provided a mini-system, we would still be losing. There isn't real value in it for them. Lenny, how much time did you waste trying to do it? Do you want to continue wasting your time?"

Lenny doesn't seem to be impressed with Gail's barrage. He simply states, "If we don't sell real value, we have a problem.

What we have to do is make sure that our product brings value to the mid-market. That's the only way out."

After a short pause, he smiles and says, "Scott, I owe you an apology. You told me that we wouldn't be able to find a comprehensive solution until we could see the product and the market simultaneously. Frankly, until now I thought that was just a rotten excuse."

"Why?" Scott is genuinely surprised.

"Those pompous words, 'the product and the market simultaneously.' Now I realize that it's exactly what you forced me to conclude. 'Making sure that our product brings value to the mid-market' is an excellent example of simultaneously considering the product and the market. I admit, you were right. Again."

Scott appreciates this.

Gail can't tolerate it anymore. "Hey fellas, back down to earth. It's one thing to state that we must provide a product that brings value. It's a totally different story to do it. You behave as if we know what this miracle product is. Correct me if I'm wrong, but I don't think that we have a clue."

"I believe that Scott does," Lenny says confidently. "Otherwise he wouldn't look like the cat that swallowed the canary. Well Scott, are you going to share the solution with us?"

"I'm afraid that your expectations are a little too high," Scott answers. "I don't have a solution. What I have, at best, is a direction towards which I hope we can find a solution. Lenny, you once told me that the problem is not the number of modules we have, the problem is that the number of features is getting out of hand."

"Correct."

"So adding one more module is something we can get away with?"

"Of course."

"Good. Now let's see where we stand. We can add one module. What should we require from that module? I think that now we know the answer to that important question. It must be a module that was an integral part of the ERP system that brings brings significant bottom-line value."

"Especially to a mid-size company," Lenny adds.

"And where are we going to find such a miracle?" Gail snaps.

"Bear with me," Scott smiles. "I know that I'm slow, but I promise that I'll reach something tangible."

"Sorry." Gail is surprised at her own impatience. Where is it coming from? It must be that her intuition is trying to warn her about something.

Scott continues. "We have concluded that due to the fact that mid-size companies are not as diverse as large companies, we can't expect that our current system will significantly decrease their inventory or increase their sales. But there are software companies promising just that. I refer to the relatively new companies offering Advanced Planning and Scheduling, or APS, as they call them."

"Oh, no. Not that again. We had talks in the past about adding finite-capacity scheduling. Aren't these APS programs based on an expansion of that kind of approach?" Gail asks.

"Basically yes," Lenny answers. "I looked into it a little. They do have something. You see, our system is based on utilizing the power of the computer to store and transfer immense amounts of data, and then being able to instantly retrieve anything that is needed. Those APS programs are based on accessing an entirely different capability of the computer. The capability to do an immense number of calculations in a very short time. They claim to optimize the entire operation, which might have a major impact on inventory and sales. I think it's time to explore that avenue in more depth. I'd have done it already if I hadn't been trapped controlling the complexity of our current system."

"Do they really bring bottom-line value?" Gail is still very skeptical.

"I don't know," Lenny admits. "As I said, I didn't have time to check."

"All their marketing is based on this claim," Scott remarks. "So, assuming that they do, I was thinking that if we integrate an APS as an additional module in our system, we can offer the market a very attractive product."

"Stressing the bottom line value will convince the conservative souls," Lenny thinks aloud, "while the overall capabilities of our system will pull all the rest.

"What do you think, Gail?" Scott asks.

"I'm not sure. Even if they do deliver bottom-line value, it's not going to be simple. Our current sales tactic is based on an alliance with the clients' Information Technology people. And this tactic becomes totally inappropriate when one tries to sell bottom-line value."

"So what?" Lenny is impatient. "Who said that our sales tactics are sacred?"

Gail prefers to ignore Lenny's statement. She knows that sales tactics are what make or break companies. You don't just gamble on a drastic change in the sales tactics. Definitely not when you have as good a tactic as BGSoft does. And you don't do it because of unfounded speculations. How can I stop this nonsense, she wonders.

Lenny is annoyed with her lack of response. "Listen Gail, if the analysis shows that . . ."

She cuts him off. "I'm not yet convinced that our analysis is correct."

"Why?" Lenny presses.

Gail knows that an answer like, 'I feel it,' will not be acceptable. To gain another second, she says, "because it's based on something that is apparently wrong."

"What do you think is wrong, Gail?" Scott asks calmly.

Like any excellent salesperson, she has learned to trust her ability to think things through on her feet. Again, it doesn't fail her. With passion in her voice, she says, "Look, you said that our system doesn't bring much value to a mid-size company. Well, this isn't true. If you don't mind, one of our smallest clients is probably our best bottom-line reference. You both know which one I'm referring to. Stein Industries. They claim that their return on investment on our system was much less than a year, and that due to our system, they have more than tripled their business in less than three years. Not one of our big clients has a return on our system that's even close."

Lenny looks at her and says, "Gosh, I know them well. Scott, she has a point."

"Unfortunately, she does," Scott admits. "We have to check what is really happening in Stein Industries."

"Important, but not urgent?" Lenny jokes.

Knowing Lenny's schedule, Scott doesn't take any chances. "No Lenny, very important and damn urgent."

Chapter 10

July 21, 1998

Stein Industries still looks pretty much the same as three years earlier when Gerald Fish, the company's CEO, initiated a move that caused them to grow from a fifty-million dollar company to over two-hundred million. For an outsider, it would be difficult to see the change. Even the sign on the CEO's office looks old. Gerald has a reputation for being very conservative with money. This reputation seems to be in conflict with the success of the company; one cannot truly succeed by saving money.

Gerald's secretary greets them heartily. "Hello, how good to see you again Lenny. You must be Maggie, welcome to our company. And you are, of course, Mr. Duncan. I've heard so much about you."

Gerald comes out of his office wearing a big friendly smile. He is surprisingly young. His beard and casual clothes are not typical of the CEOs they usually do business with. He shakes hands first with Maggie. "Hello, Maggie, I think this is your first visit to Stein Industries. Please come inside," he says, shaking hands with Scott and Lenny.

This is no longer a small company, thinks Scott. But it feels like one, warm and informal. I don't sense the tension and pressure of a company going through accelerated growth.

As if to answer his thoughts, someone rushes through the door. Upon seeing Gerald with guests, he stops abruptly and turns to retreat.

"Roger, wait a minute. Meet three outstanding people who are responsible for our great information system," says Gerald.

Roger shakes hands with them.

"Roger is our key dispatcher guy. He sees to it that every shipment goes out on time. Now, when he comes to me it means something needs to be delayed. Is that right, Roger?"

"Well, not exactly. Lucifer asked if we could ship their order so they get it by eight A.M. I went over the night-shift plan with Jane, and we can squeeze it in if I call two trucks for midnight. I looked for Jimmy for approval but he's on his way to San Diego. I didn't know you had guests."

Maggie laughs loudly. "What company calls itself 'Lucifer'?"

Roger is embarrassed. "Oh, no ma'am, that's not their name, we call them that 'cause they're so mean."

Gerald smiles and says to Roger, "Don't worry, Lucifer will pay for the special delivery. Their controller promised me last week that they'd honor any invoice for urgent delivery. I think they've learned their lesson."

In addition to the friendliness and informality, there is also a feeling of calm and camaraderie, Scott realizes. They enter Gerald's private office.

"Delighted to have all of you here. What an honor. However, I assume you usually visit customers who have complaints. We don't."

They chuckle. Scott picks up the ball. "Gerald, you personally presented at our user group conference two years ago. You declared that BGSoft beautifully supported your business. You even said that your investment in the whole application was fully returned in much less than a year. We'd naturally like to hear more about it."

Gerald laughs. "It's about time you showed some interest.

Let me guess. Not that many of your customers have such an impressive return on your software?"

"That's right."

"Well," Gerald begins, "please don't take this personally, but I don't buy technology just because everybody else is buying it. Or because it's nice or sophisticated. I buy technology for only one reason."

He pauses to stress his point. "I buy technology only when I'm convinced I can make more money by using it.

"Luckily for us, not every president has the same opinion," Maggie comments half jokingly. Whoa! she thinks, this guy's friendly, relaxed manner is contagious.

Gerald flashes a smile at her. "So, several years ago I had a very clear idea of how your system could help me make profits. Frankly, at the start it didn't work out as I expected, but eventually we made it work. Since then the software has played an important part in our business."

They wait for him to continue, but he doesn't.

"We came here for the details," Scott gently reminds him.

"You want the details?" Gerald checks. "I'm not sure that I want my competitors to know the details. Okay, let me give you the basics."

"That's what we're here for," Maggie assures him.

"My interest in your ERP system started around . . . mid nineteen ninety-five. That year started out as a bad one for Stein Industries. We were not yet losing money, but I saw it coming. In nineteen ninety-four there had been a small decline in the market and in 'ninety-five it intensified. We were too damn near break-even. I was concerned because it looked like the decline would continue. For us, further decline meant being in a spot that's difficult to bounce back from. We desperately needed more sales."

He pauses, remembering how hard it was to think proactively, how hard it was to resist the temptation to seek refuge in "right-sizing."

"I was looking for a competitive edge. That was the only

way we could survive the decline without losing too many of our people. So, I tried to analyze the situation through the eyes of my customers. I knew I had to find something that was really important for them. Once I put my mind to it, it wasn't too difficult to zero in on the critical factor.

"Our customers deal with large projects. Our products come relatively late in the game; when a client comes to us, their project is near completion. This is the only way they can give us the precise measurements we need. No wonder that often, completion of the whole project has to wait for our product. So I thought, what if I could promise much faster delivery than my competitors?"

He pauses and asks, "Got the picture?"

"Are you kidding?" Maggie smiles. "It's the story of my life, my implementations. The final stage of our projects is always testing the new system while still working with the legacy systems. It hurts the performance of the company, and the frustration goes up sharply. Don't worry, Gerald, we can easily relate to pressures near the end of a project."

Scott pushes on. "Your point is clear, Gerald. Fast and reliable response from you is of the utmost importance to your customers. Cutting your lead time should give you a competitive edge. So you decided that ERP technology could do it for you."

"Not so fast, not so fast. First of all, please call me Gerry. And yes, Scott, you're right, I wanted to cut lead times. I was aware that ERP companies claimed their systems reduced lead time, but I didn't take it for granted. Not at all. I had to be sure that whatever we did would work. Besides, I don't have money to throw around.

"I put together a team to check our process, and find out how we could cut the lead time. The team found that preproduction, especially the price quotation part, took almost two weeks. They also found that every order was delayed at least another week because of material shortages. Once those two causes were revealed, the option of ERP was raised. That's a big step for a company our size, and we hadn't really considered it before.

"We knew that an ERP system could help us shorten the time it takes to do the price quote. We also knew that it could help us better manage the materials, reducing the problem with shortages. Based on this, I estimated that using ERP, we could shorten the lead time from an average of ten weeks to about seven.

"Of course, before investing such enormous sums of money, I wanted to make sure I could get more sales. I visited all my big customers. Based on what they told me, I felt I could safely say that reducing our lead time to seven weeks would give us at least ten percent more sales. I needed the sales so badly, and the chance looked so good, that I made the decision to purchase your system for the huge price you charged."

"Good decision," says Maggie. Not too sophisticated, she thinks. But, she realizes, his rationale was straight bottom-line justification. And they also saved on cost since the misers did the implementation themselves.

"Did you have any problems installing the system?" she asks.

"Not really," Gerry says flatly. "It even worked as we expected. Within a relatively short time we were able to cut the preproduction from two weeks to two days, and very few orders were delayed due to shortages."

"Nice success story," Maggie concludes.

"Who's talking about success?" Gerry grins. "It was a total failure."

It's his day. At last the big kahunas have recognized that he has done something very different. And he intends to squeeze every drop of satisfaction from it.

"The system worked. Lead time went down. The concept seems right; you should have gotten the sales lift. So what happened?" asks Scott.

"The system worked, but the lead time did not go down," Gerry answers.

"I don't understand." Maggie is puzzled. "But you said . . ."

"Yes, I know what I said. And at the time, believe me, I was as puzzled as you are, if not more. You see, in my business, if I go and commit to seven weeks and then don't deliver in seven weeks, or at the most eight, I'm out of business. So, of course, before committing to our clients, we tested. Well, we finished preproduction in just two days all right, there were no material shortages to speak of, but we were still scrambling to ship the order in ten weeks."

"How come?"

"Yes, that was exactly my question."

Lenny thinks that the problem is somewhat familiar. In his days working with MRP, he came to realize that giving production more time didn't improve the ability to ship on time, or reduce expediting.

Gerry continues. "Sometime later, my operations manager and I attended a Constraint's Management symposium. One presentation was given by this guy talking about their TOC implementation in production. I couldn't believe my ears; he was describing our environment, even though he was from a very different industry. He proved that in conventional complicated operations like ours, releasing the work earlier does not mean that it will come out the other end earlier. Releasing more work orders means that queues grow, and the average time to complete each work order grows!"

He pauses, letting them digest that, and then continues. "That explained why we hadn't seen any results. What happened was that the two weeks saved on preproduction were actually used to release the materials to the plant two weeks earlier. Thus, the shop floor now contained ten weeks of work rather than eight. The foremen, faced with more work orders, had more decisions to make, and many more possibilities for mistakes. Eventually, all the allotted time was fully used—exactly as Parkinson's Law claims."

Gerry looks at his audience. They're with him. They might be big shots, but they're learning new stuff from him.

"So, our problem was to complete every order in seven weeks, rather than ten. The presenter we saw suggested using the Drum-Buffer-Rope method. In its crudest form it just means choking the material release according to the orders' due dates; delaying the release of work orders until seven weeks before their final due date.

"I must admit, that at the time, it sounded counter-intuitive to me. It meant we had an order, we had the materials, the work centers at the start of the process had nothing to do, and yet we don't release the work. I understood the argument that releasing the order earlier meant it'd be stuck downstream causing traffic jams and confusion. But to accept that in order to finish earlier, it had to release later, was hard.

"Jane, my operations manager, was convinced we should do it. So, I let her try. And of course it worked—we could safely deliver every order in seven weeks."

"So you instructed your sales agents to quote seven weeks delivery. And sales started to roll in." Scott completes the picture.

"This move brought us almost twenty percent more sales," Gerry confirms. "Now we were making money. We were off the hook. And . . . I had time to think about the next step."

Gerry pauses, staring at his guests.

Scott smiles. He is aware Gerry wants him to try to guess. "If you could release the orders seven weeks before delivery and make it, why not try six weeks, or even less?"

Gerry acknowledges the remark with a smile. "Absolutely right. But I approached it from a different angle. My clients wanted shorter lead times because they get real value from it. If I'm the only one who provides it, why shouldn't I share in this value? Why not get higher prices?

"I wanted to continue the strategy of gaining more market by cutting the lead time. But I introduced another element. I wanted to get more money for the increased value I generate for the customer.

"My idea was to offer an option of four-week delivery for an additional ten percent on top of the regular price. I thought that such an offer would be attractive to many of our clients. Besides, being able to make such an offer would build our reputation—put us in a breed apart."

"Of course, with such an offer you needed to ensure ninety-nine percent on-time delivery," Lenny remarks.

"Right. By then we were familiar with TOC, and we studied the Drum-Buffer-Rope planning technique in detail. We thought we knew how to safely achieve another quantum leap in our lead times. We needed to drastically reduce the queue and wait times. For that we needed to carefully schedule our most loaded resource, and synchronize the material release schedule accordingly. I asked the team to design the Drum-Buffer-Rope planning process in detail.

"After a week, they reported they had a problem. Scheduling the bottleneck could be done manually. But then, to ensure synchronization of the release of our hundreds of materials, we needed the ERP system. So we needed to connect the bottleneck schedule to the ERP."

Lenny continues the story from his perspective. "Now I understand your request for the code change. You wanted me to add a feature that accepts a detailed schedule for a certain resource and implodes to calculate the effect on the orders' completion dates. I was wondering about this odd request. It was counter to what ERP/MRP algorithms usually do. I read one or two books on Drum-Buffer-Rope planning but didn't make the obvious connection."

Gerry nods. "You are quite right. The best solution was to ask you to write that small feature. When your price quote for one-hundred-thousand dollars came to me, I was furious. That was a very small feature to program! Don't tell me otherwise."

Scott laughs. "I remember the incident. Lenny insisted that only he could do it . . . And it was so special that we couldn't use it anywhere else. So I gave you that quote. As a matter of fact, I hoped you would back off. Lenny was so busy that his time was more precious to us than the hundred thousand."

Gerry smiles. "I almost cancelled that request. I thought of using an Excel model to do it. Luckily my production manager convinced me that for all practical purposes it was impossible; we really needed that feature embedded in the ERP software. She reminded me we intended to make a small fortune from it. That was pretty convincing.

"Once we got the additional feature we went into action." Gerry continues the story. "The announcement that we were accepting four-week orders made us quite famous. Our sales went up sharply. By focusing on the bottleneck we could improve its performance. That was very valuable because we found we could do more with the same people than we had ever imagined. When sales took off even more we had to go to night shifts on the bottleneck and two other work centers pretty regularly.

"Still, I was frustrated by the reluctance of my customers to pay the extra ten percent. With my largest customers it ended up at a mere two percent. We were doing great, but those misers made me furious."

Look who's talking, Maggie smiles to herself.

Lenny encourages Gerry. "You came last year with another strange request . . ."

Gerry continues. "Yes, as I said, my mind was on the market. I still wanted to get much more money for much more value to the customer. The four-week delivery option was good, but not enough for our customers to pay significantly more. I asked myself, under what circumstances would they be willing to pay us any price we asked?"

"When a last minute problem arises, and one part is holding up the whole project," Maggie confidently answers.

"Exactly!" Gerry looks at her with new appreciation. "So I realized that me making a clear commitment that whenever a client has a real problem, we are willing to deliver an urgent order even with just a week's notice, is a very attractive safety net for our clients. A thirty percent surcharge on urgent orders is not an issue. Of course, I was willing to give this offer only to customers who promise all their business to us.

"There was only one little problem. I gathered the team and all my key people, and asked them one question: how can we ship up to a quarter of all our orders in one week, and still not miss any due dates?"

"And what did they say?" Maggie asks.

"They said it was 'totally impossible! Completely out of the question!' I liked this answer because that would be the reaction of our competitors as well. I simply asked them to keep thinking."

"You have a lot of confidence in your peoples' ability," Scott says.

"Yes, I do," Gerry assures him. He smiles. "And I knew that they knew where to look for the solution."

"Buffer-Management?" Lenny asks.

"Exactly."

In answer to Scott's unspoken question, Lenny explains. "It's the follow-on step of the Drum-Buffer-Rope. When you want to squeeze lead times to the extent that they start to approach the magnitude of delays caused by Murphy . . ."

"You mean," Maggie tries to understand, "something like a machine breakdown?"

"Basically, yes," Gerry takes over. "But I'm more concerned with the more routine things. You see, in our company it's unusual for a machine to go down for more than a day, but it's very common for a work order to be stuck in some queue for two, or even three days. When you want a substantial number of orders to be completed in just one week, your operation must know how to handle it. On the one hand, you must frequently jump the queue, but on the other, if you constantly juggle the production plan you throw your operation into chaos. The answer is to supplement the planning system with an execution system.

"We run our Drum-Buffer-Rope system only once a week, and we stick to the resulting plan. Of course we leave enough spare capacity on the bottleneck so that urgent orders do not disrupt the plan, they are just added to it. The material release and the work of the bottleneck always obey the planned schedule.

"In addition, we have Buffer-Management running on line. Based on the planned schedule and feedback from some key work centers, it provides everybody with what's most important to them."

He leans forward. "This is key. Everybody, including the support functions, looks at the buffers all the time. Whenever anybody has a queue, has a choice about what to do next, they look at the buffers."

"I can lend you my books on Buffer-Management if you're interested," Lenny says to the other two.

"I am," says Scott. "The concept of an execution system as distinct from the planning is new to me," he confesses.

"That's the problem," Gerry groans. "That's why we had to pay you another fortune for your programmers to help us develop it."

"Lenny, were you personally involved?"

"No, he wasn't," Gerry answers. "And you didn't charge me an arm and a leg for the programming work itself. You just charged me for having more people connected on line. Believe me, if my people hadn't proved to me that it's essential to be fully integrated with the ERP system, I would never have agreed to pay you for so many more concurrent users. I still don't understand why I had to pay you so much."

"Have you made money out of it?" Scott asks, smiling.

"You bet," Gerry grins again. "You, Scott, are very proud of forty percent growth every year. I think we'll grow this year by another seventy-five percent."

Scott leans forward. "This is very impressive, Gerry. What's your next step?"

Gerry laughs. "Oh, Scott. You don't expect me to tell you that."

*   *   *

The first question Scott asks after they enter their limo is, "Lenny, under what type of contract did you write the code for Gerald?"

"It's Gerry, remember? But if you're asking who holds the copyrights? We do."

"Good. And how tailored is that code?" Scott continues questioning.

"There are parts which are totally tailored," Lenny answers. "But most is generic. To answer your real question, for Drum-Buffer-Rope, based on this code, I can provide a good enough program within a few weeks. To turn it into a package that can be used in any environment is another story. Something between six months and a year."

"That's for planning. What about the execution part?"

"The Buffer-Management piece? I don't know. I have to check what we did there, but it can't be that big a job." Lenny doesn't seem overly concerned.

"Maybe I can save you the time," Maggie interjects. "Scott, why all these questions? What are you getting at?"

"Isn't it obvious," Scott replies. "We have the answer for the mid-range market."

"I don't think so," Maggie says firmly.

Scott tries to persuade her. "Look, Maggie, Gerry represents our sales-peoples' nightmare. He's cheap, he's not impressed with technology, and he's small. Not a prospect you could expect to turn into a client. Certainly not as good a client as he is."

"And the key is value," Lenny joins in. "Maggie, we said that the key to the mid-market is value, bottom-line value. Now we know how to provide it."

"No we don't," Maggie says emphatically.

If they didn't respect her opinions they would ignore her. But since it's Maggie, they listen.

"Between the two of you, you probably know everything there is to know about computer systems for business."

"After today, I'm not sure anymore," Scott mutters.

She ignores his remark and continues, "But when it comes to implementation, to working with the people who have to use the system, to overcoming suspicion and resistance, I think I've learned a thing or two. Friends, don't you realize that sweet-talkin', innocent Gerry didn't tell us the full story?"

"What didn't he tell us?"

"He didn't tell us how difficult it was to install the system. I don't mean to install on the computer, I mean to install it in his peoples' heads. Don't you realize that what he described to us was actually a culture change? No, a cultural revolution!"

When she sees that they're not impressed, she tries to explain it from another angle. "Look, changing the rules is tough. People are threatened by change. He told us how he felt about choking the release of orders. How awkward it was to have the order, to have the material, to have the people free, and nevertheless not to release the work. He told us how he felt. What do you think his people felt?

"What do you think people feel when they are not being fed enough work? Don't you realize that the question that starts to go through their heads is 'when are they going to announce the layoffs?' To achieve full collaboration under such circumstances is not a triviality.

"This guy not only had the intelligence and insight to create these solutions for his company, he must be an amazing manager to have gotten his people to go along with him."

Scott recalls the impression of trust and good feelings within the company. Even the guy from shipping seemed comfortable talking with his CEO.

Maggie continues, "You know that changing the technology is often met with hostility. Don't you realize that when you change to something that conflicts with the performance-measurement system you may run into a wall?"

"Of course we do." Scott is not happy. "But what does the performance-measurement system have to do with what Gerald told us."

"I'm not aware of any change that Stein Industries made to our performance-measurement module," Lenny confirms.

"You've been looking at the world through the lenses of your computer systems for too long." Maggie knows she's not reaching them. But she is not the type to give up. "Listen guys, do you agree that worker efficiency is part of the performance-measurement system?"

"Yes," Lenny has no problem agreeing.

"When the release of material is synchronized to the bottle-neck schedule, what must happen to the efficiencies of all the workers who man the non-bottlenecks? Gerry never even mentioned 'efficiencies,' but I'm telling you, for the method he described to work, he had to chase out the efficiency measurement from Stein Industries. I bet he had wars with his employees on that issue alone."

"I see," says Lenny.

"You're right," Scott admits. "The change Gerry succeeded in implementing is by far more substantial than what he actually said.

"It explains another thing. I wondered why he didn't hesitate to reveal all the technical details to us. Now it's clear. Due to these difficulties Maggie described, he knows that it will be almost impossible for his competitors to imitate."

"Precisely," Maggie agrees.

"And that's bad news for us," Scott is quick to grasp.

"Why?" Lenny asks.

"Suppose that you write the code," Scott explains. "What are the chances that it will be implemented, including the essential culture change, so it will bring value?"

"Maggie's people can take care of the required culture change," Lenny suggests.

"Not a chance," Maggie retorts. "My people are experts in system integration. But to bring about a culture change, they are about as qualified as your programmers are."

The last argument convinces Lenny. "So what are we going to do?"

"What you have already decided to do," Maggie says decisively. "If the problem is that there are traffic jams on the shop floor, we don't have to change all the rules. We just need a very smart traffic cop."

"You mean an optimization program, adding an APS module?"

"That is exactly what I mean," Maggie answers.

"Fine," Scott says. And he starts to hum.

Chapter 11

July 27, 1998

Monday 8:30 A.M. Lenny is tired as hell, as he enters the offices of Intelogic, one of the best APS companies. He's still furious at the airline company who kept them in the plane for about three hours looking for some technical failure before they finally took off. He hadn't reached his hotel until three in the morning. The combination of fatigue and fury has made him very impatient.

He introduces himself to Lora, the administrative manager of Intelogic. She is expecting him. Lenny is casually dressed, his hair is not combed, and his shaving is uneven, giving him an overall unkempt appearance. Hardly the look of a senior executive.

Masking her disappointment, she greets him cordially. "Glad to see you here, sir. Chuck Monroe will walk you through our software, and at twelve-thirty Keith Miller, our VP of Sales, would like to have lunch with you. Let me take you to Chuck's office."

All Chuck was told was that someone from BGSoft would like to see the Intelogic software. When Lenny walks through the door, Chuck quickly deduces from his appearance that Lenny is neither in business development nor in marketing or sales. He wonders about Lenny's exact objective. Lacking any clear direction, Chuck gambles on doing the routine presentation about the software. He starts with the regular sales pitch about today's competition, and the need to replace inventory with information.

Lenny, realizing that he's talking to a salesman, asks him to skip the nonsense. "What is the objective function of the software?"

Chuck replies automatically, "Optimization throughout the supply chain. Lead-time reductions, inventory reduction, more efficient use of resources, improved on-time delivery, and improved customer service by immediate order quotation."

Lenny detests people who just quote from a sales brochure. In a sharp tone he retorts, "How does the software reduce inventory while improving the efficiency of resources?"

"Very good question," Chuck answers. "This is exactly why you need such clever APS software. This is a true finite-capacity scheduler, so the capacity is carefully monitored and planned. Let me show you the program."

Lenny, trying to control his impatience, says, "I've already seen a demo of the software. I even brought my own data. But, before I ask you to load my data, I wish to know more about the concepts behind the algorithm. Who can tell me about that?"

Chuck begins to realize that this is not his day. The routine sales pitch is not going to work on this guy—whoever he is. He tries to discreetly and professionally get rid of Lenny. Chuck is already thinking about the other sales opportunities that he could be working on right now. "You probably need to look for someone from Engineering, but I'm not sure anybody is available right now. And the algorithms behind the software are our proprietary secrets. And I'm sorry, but we're not allowed to load customer files into our computers. Only the software engineers are authorized to do that. This is management policy because of all the viruses."

Lenny gets up. "OK, Chuck, thank you." He goes back to Lora at the central office. She's on the phone. He leans towards her. She says, "I'll call you back," hangs up, and sends Lenny a questioning look.

"Sorry to bother you. There's some misunderstanding here. I came from BGSoft to get an in-depth look at your software. Chuck definitely can't help me with that. I was under the impression I would meet your VP of Development, or whatever his title is. Can you find out when I can speak with him?"

Lora only raises her eyebrows. She remains cool and cordial. "Our VP of Sales, Mr. Miller, is going to meet you at lunchtime. I don't think Mr. Bell, the VP of Engineering, is available at the moment."

Lenny nods. "I see. Can you please tell Don Hanson that Lenny from BGSoft wants a quick word with him."

Lora's calm is now broken. Don Hanson is Intelogic's president.

"Please sit down Mr. Abrahms. I'll see what I can do."

Lenny sits in the leather armchair at the corner of the office. After several seconds Don Hanson strides into the room.

"Lenny, I'm so glad to have you here. I talked to Scott about you coming to check us out. Somehow I wasn't notified you were coming today. I apologize for the misunderstanding."

Don turns to Lora.

"Is Chris in his office?"

"Yes. He's conducting his weekly meeting with the team managers."

"Good. That means that Dinesh is with him. Let Chris know that Lenny Abrahms from BGSoft and I are coming down to his office. Now."

Lora picks up the phone. Don turns to Lenny.

"I wish I could sit with you myself, but right now I have some people from China in my office. Chris Bell is our VP of Engineering, and I believe at this stage, you would be more interested in talking to him than to me. Let me take you to his office."

Don walks Lenny to the elevator. While they are going up, Don tells Lenny that Engineering is quite busy polishing the new version announced for release in a month. The new version adds the financial aspects to the global optimization. Lenny wonders about the accuracy of their release schedules. Hopefully it's better than the airline last night.

Just as the door of the elevator opens, Chris Bell, vaguely familiar to Lenny, comes down the corridor to welcome them. He is followed closely by another guy.

"Lenny, let me introduce Chris Bell, our VP of Engineering, and our chief scientist Dinesh Nagpal. I'm sure Lenny Abrahms needs no introduction."

"Hello, Lenny," Chris says as they shake hands. "We have met briefly on several occasions. Great to have you here. Meet Dinesh. He is the chief mind behind our optimization methods. He holds a PhD in Math from Cornell."

"I see that I'm now in good hands," Lenny says to Don. "I know you have to go back to your guests."

They sit down in Chris's office. Lenny opens his laptop case and pulls out a diskette. "This contains a small case study I've done for this occasion. You have it here in two formats, in Access and as a text file. Can you import one of these to Intelogic?"

Chris smiles. "No problem. Dinesh, can you see to that? I'm curious to see the details of the case."

Dinesh turns to the computer, inserts the diskette, and imports the case into the Intelogic system. Dinesh then uses the Display Options to get the hang of the case. Lenny reviews some of the details with them.

Chris laughs as some of the complexities are revealed. "I see you have prepared an interesting case study for us. I love it."

Lenny explains. "This is not a fictional case. This is a much simplified version of a real company I worked with about twenty years ago. Of course, the computer system at that time was pretty primitive, so I had to know every detail by heart in order to force the system to do the right things. Now, before we start, what should I expect to get?"

Dinesh answers, "The first objective is to see that all the customer orders can be shipped on time, considering material availability, capacity constraints, and tool availability. This is the most important objective."

He runs the program. In seconds they get a split screen with blinking data lines.

Chris proudly says, "In almost no time the optimizer considers all the data and comes up with the best practical schedule for every product, material, and work center. Exactly what has to be done, when, and by whom. What is now displayed is the essential summary; the result of following this schedule."

Lenny is not particularly impressed. The example is relatively small, and today's computers are powerful. What will impress him is not speed, but rather the quality of the results.

He listens attentively to Dinesh's more explicit explanation. "What we see here," he points to the left of the screen, "is that the optimizer identified three bottlenecks. In other words, these three work centers simply don't have enough capacity to process all the orders on time. Therefore, unless we add this much to capacity, some of the orders will be delayed relative to their promised due dates.

"What we see here," Dinesh moves his finger to the right of the screen, "is the new Master Schedule with the updated shipping dates. The two blinking lines are the two orders that will not finish on time. You see, one is going to be delayed by four days and the other by twelve."

"This is one of the big advantages of the software," Chris says proudly. "It tells you in advance what problems you are going to face, so you have enough time to take corrective action."

Lenny leans forward so he can better read the information displayed. After a short while he remarks, "I see that most orders will finish ahead of time. A few are scheduled to finish way ahead of time."

"Yes," says Chris. "The optimizer minimized the impact of not having enough capacity to affect only those two orders."

"But," Lenny wonders aloud, "can't we schedule it that, for

example, this order will not finish so early, and use the capacity to reduce the delay on the two late orders?"

"Apparently not," Chris says confidently. "This is the best practical schedule."

"How do I know that?" Lenny asks.

Lenny knows that to construct a schedule is not a big deal. To construct a good schedule is. To construct the best schedule has been declared by mathematicians to be an unsolved problem. That is probably why Intelogic is careful to state that they provide the best practical schedule. Since no one has defined what "practical" is, they can get away with it. Lenny will be happy with a good schedule, but he is not ready to just take their word for it.

As he expected, Dinesh is the one to answer, but his answer is not what Lenny expects. "Do you want me," Dinesh says, "to print the detailed schedules of all the work centers? Do you want to try and verify for yourself that it is impossible to improve on one of the two late orders without creating bigger damage to the other orders?"

Lenny doesn't like Dinesh's suggestion. As a matter of fact, he regards it as a blatant attempt to deceive him. Controlling his impatience, Lenny says, "Even on my relatively small example there are enough variables to cause the number of possible schedules to be astronomical. How much time do I have to invest in doing what you are suggesting? A year?"

Dinesh doesn't answer.

Lenny doesn't like it. They are the ones claiming that Intelogic schedule is the best practical schedule. Rightfully, Lenny expects that they will provide a proof for their claim rather then sending him on a wild goose chase.

Realizing that Dinesh and Chris are not going to offer a way to really check the quality of their software, Lenny has no choice but to do it himself.

"Can you consider a situation where machines have to be idle for maintenance?" he asks.

"Of course," says Chris. "Intelogic is capable of taking maintenance into account in whatever way you want. This is one of the strengths of our software. It can mirror the reality of almost any plant."

"So it will not be a problem to schedule one-day maintenance on one of the bottlenecks?"

"Not at all," Chris assures him. Then he realizes that Lenny would like it to be done now. "Dinesh?"

Rather than making the necessary change, Dinesh comments, "To deal with the late orders we should give more capacity, what you're asking for will do the exact opposite."

"I understand," Lenny answers.

Dinesh looks as if he wants to argue, but seeing Lenny's determined face, he turns to the keyboard.

"What I'm expecting," Lenny says, "is that reducing one day on a bottleneck will cause the two late orders to be delayed by another day, and some of the early orders will not be as early."

"You already ran it? Good. Now let's see what we've got."

One of the two late orders is not late any more. Instead another order is late.

Lenny's face hardens. "Can you explain this?" he asks Dinesh.

"You have eliminated a day on the bottleneck and that is the result. That's the best that can be done in the situation that you have dictated." Dinesh says flatly.

"Dinesh, you keep on telling me that 'that's the best.' You don't give any proof, you just claim it. Why should I take your word for it when the result that I see doesn't make sense. Look, the data didn't contain any information about the price of the orders or the relative importance of the clients. So, juggling the orders' completion dates around was done for no good reason. Can you explain it?"

Chris comes to the rescue. "Lenny, this is what is so good about the software. The downtime for maintenance is noted, and a new schedule is generated. So from that you can see that when things do not go as planned, when you lose time due to unexpected problems, you can run Intelogic again, and you'll get a new schedule which tells you the best you can do to meet the due dates. Of course, when too many failures occur, you may have to add overtime. Intelogic will lead you to recognize that need."

Lenny has had it. "Listen guys, stop trying to jerk me around! I'm trying to check the quality of the schedule and you ignore my questions and give me a sales pitch! Can we talk straight? I'm not a prospect that you're persuading to buy a copy of the software."

"You are much more important than a regular prospect," Chris says, trying to pacify Lenny. "We know that you didn't come to buy one copy of our software. If anything you came to buy the entire company."

"And you don't want to be bought?"

"On the contrary," Chris answers with a straight face. "There is nothing I would like more than becoming a multi-million-aire. And besides, I'd love to belong to a company with endless resources to invest in further development."

"If that's the case," Lenny says gently, "let me give you some advice." Looking directly at Dinesh he says, "Be as frank as you can with me."

Dinesh's color deepens.

"Let's cut to the chase," Lenny says. "What gives you the confidence that the schedules that Intelogic generates are even good?"

If Dinesh starts to run on about the algorithm, Lenny decides he will give up and leave. There are many other APS companies. As it turns out, he doesn't have to write off the day because Dinesh is no longer trying to put up a smokescreen.

"There are two reasons." Dinesh answers. "The first is that I spent a lot of time trying to match myself against Intelogic. The current version beats me every time. I know that doesn't say much . . ."

"It says a lot," Lenny encourages him. Dinesh's color is returning to normal. "What's the second reason?"

"I've tested the results against other APS packages. Most are not even coming close, and no one gives better results."

It is unclear what criteria Dinesh used to compare the packages, but from his body language, it is apparent that he is reporting his true impression. That's good enough for Lenny. Intelogic schedules are not the best possible schedules but they are probably the best an APS computer system can give. Is it good enough? Will they bring enough value to its users?

"Dinesh, can you explain to me why the results of the second run was so dramatically different from the first run?"

"It's the nature of the beast," is the answer. "Look, what is the meaning of an optimized schedule? We are trying, as much as possible, to schedule everything back-to-back. That's the only way to maximize capacity utilization and to minimize lead time. So when a resource has finished a task, the software attempts to schedule it to immediately start another task. When one task is finished on a work order, the software attempts to schedule the next task on that work order to start as soon as possible.

"Now you can see what must happen when you change the starting conditions. Suppose that the change is minimal. It is restricted to one work order being a little bit delayed. This change is now spreading to other work orders and to other resources. Simply, since we cannot afford resources standing idle, the resource that would be assigned to our work order is now assigned to another work order. Likewise, the assignment of another resource, the one that is supposed to do the next task on our work order, will have to change, and so on. The change is spreading to the entire operation."

Lenny knew all that before he came. Therefore he doesn't have any difficulty stating the not so trivial conclusion. "That means that the less spare capacity in operations, the more unstable the schedules become."

"Unfortunately, that is the case," Dinesh confirms with a nod.

Lenny decides to move on. As he expected, the APS software

products schedules are not the "practical" best, and they are unstable. But the schedules that plants are following, schedules that are generated by reacting to demands and surprises, also suffer from those problems. So it is still possible that using Intelogic will bring benefits to a plant. To increase his chances of checking it is essential to preserve Chris's, and even more so, Dinesh's openness and collaboration.

"Accepting that Intelogic is one of the best APS packages available," Lenny says, "please regard my next questions in the proper light. Do not take them as criticism on Intelogic, but as a sincere attempt at understanding the value of APS packages in general."

"We understand," Dinesh says graciously.

"I understand that in most cases, the user is adding capacity until all orders are scheduled to finish at or before their respective due dates?"

Dinesh is careful now. "Correct," he says. But to make sure that Lenny does not misinterpret, he clarifies. "Of course, the user will not add capacity to the point that all orders finish ahead of time. He will do it only up to the point that most orders will finish on time or with an insignificant delay. Don't forget that the second objective of Intelogic is to increase the efficiency of utilizing the existing capacity."

"That's what I thought," says Lenny. "Now we know that Murphy exists. That we cannot realistically expect that reality will precisely follow our plan. That disruptions constantly occur on the shop floor, that . . ."

"Of course," Dinesh cuts the string of repetitions. "That's reality."

"With that in mind," Lenny continues, "would you say that your schedule is realistic?"

"What do you mean?" asks Chris.

"If at least one order, and probably many more, are scheduled to finish exactly on the day they are due," Lenny explains, "then due to delays caused by Murphy they will not finish on time. If this is the case, then Intelogic's promised due dates are not realistic."

"Well, this is not entirely true," Dinesh objects. "Most users put more liberal time estimates, some safety time, into their data. These safety times reduce the severity of that problem."

"But doesn't putting more liberal time estimates negate Intelogic's second objective? Doesn't it reduce the ability to use resources efficiently?"

"It also increases inventory and elongates the lead times," Dinesh says, enhancing Lenny's argument. "But most users see it as a trade-off. The more safety time added, the more reliable the schedule is, but the less effective resource utilization is."

Lenny sees now a possible way in which the APS can bring real value. "Dinesh," he says thoughtfully, "you have much more experience than I do at optimizing schedules. Isn't it true that the same amount of safety time when inserted in one stage of the process can help much more than if it is inserted in another stage?"

"Yes, it is," Dinesh confirms. "For example, inserting safety time right before a bottleneck is much more effective than inserting it in other places. But the bottlenecks may move."

"If that's the case, can a user of Intelogic specify the total amount of safety time he is willing to give and have the software insert it in the right places? This might give much better schedules than can be done manually."

"No," Dinesh answers flatly. "Intelogic does not do that."

This is too important for Lenny to drop the issue. "Why?" he asks.

"Because we handle this issue in a much better way," comes the triumphant answer. "You see, we don't ignore the fact that Murphy will cause problems. But we also do not recommend inserting safety times. When there is a disruption, like a machine breakdown, or if a vendor doesn't deliver on time, the user should rerun Intelogic. He will get a new optimized schedule.

"Optimized" Lenny thinks to himself. We have already established that Intelogic schedules are not optimized, they are not even exceptionally good. Forget it, he tells himself. Listen to what the man has to say.

Dinesh continues, "If the disruption is severe the software recommends adding capacity. As you've seen, it tells you on which work center overtime is needed and exactly how much. We don't use safety time to protect the schedule. It's too expensive. We use safety capacity."

The last sentence triggers Lenny's interest. That is an interesting approach," he comments. He tries to examine it. "Safety *TIME* must be added before the disruption occurs, and it might not occur at all. That means that whether or not Murphy hits, the penalty was paid; inventory and lead time have increased. But with safety *CAPACITY*, the user decides on it only after the disruption occurs. So the amount of overtime used is exactly the amount needed. Smart."

Dinesh looks smug.

Lenny adds, "This might be of value to any plant."

Chris now feels confident enough to add, "You are right. This is the biggest advantage of Intelogic. Every time there is a deviation from the plan, simply rerun and you'll get the new optimized schedule. This is our strongest selling point. The speed of the software is so remarkable that the user can even do it every hour."

Lenny ignores Chris and continues. "But I see a major problem. If I understood you correctly you suggest rerunning the software every time there's a disturbance."

"Maybe not every time," Dinesh tries to protect the feasibility of his approach. "But the more frequent the better."

Lenny is troubled by something much more fundamental. "Didn't we say that almost any change in the situation, even a small change, results in a reshuffling of the schedule?"

"Yes."

"And that doesn't bother you?"

"Why should it?"

"Because reshuffling of the schedule of everybody means

that we helped a local disturbance, a local problem, spread to the whole plant."

Dinesh doesn't respond.

"Doesn't it bother you?" Lenny is surprised. "If we institute a mechanism that helps to spread the impact of local disturbance, we might jeopardize the performance of the system much more than we help it. If we help any small blip, anywhere, to tangibly affect the work of everybody in the plant, we turn random noise into deterministic deviations. We both know that such a thing might throw the whole plant into chaos. It's basic statistics." He stops and looks at Dinesh for an answer.

"I've thought about it," Dinesh says.

"Of course you did. What is your conclusion?"

"You said that 'we might throw the plant into chaos.' The word 'might' is the key word in your argument."

"Yes," says Lenny. "But you know that the nature of the dependencies in a plant causes the individual delays to accumulate. There are many articles about it. So the chance of throwing the plant into chaos is high. As a matter of fact, the more I think about it, the more I'm convinced that it's almost guaranteed."

"No, Lenny. It does not happen."

Lenny is willing to let himself be convinced by Dinesh. But he needs proof.

"What prevents it from happening? What dumps the accumulation of the delays?" he asks, waiting to hear the logical, or at least the mathematical, proof.

"It simply does not happen," Dinesh says confidently. "Our clients are reporting excellent results."

For the last twenty years Lenny has worked in the real world, so for him this is a very strong argument. But he also learned how careful one must be with such arguments. "What is the correlation between the frequency of running Intelogic and the improvement in your customers' results?" he asks.

Dinesh doesn't answer.

Lenny realizes that Chris, in order to let Dinesh concentrate on his work, is probably shielding him from the field. Lenny turns to Chris and repeats his question. "A customer that runs Intelogic every hour, how much does his performance improve relative to a customer that runs Intelogic only once a day?"

"I don't know," Chris admits. "As a matter of fact, I doubt if we have any customer that runs our software every hour. Most run it only once a week."

Dinesh looks at Chris with surprise.

Well, Lenny thinks, back to the drawing board. Aloud he asks, "Can I get a list of your customers who report the best results?"

"Of course," Chris assures him. "Keith Miller, our VP of Sales, who you are meeting for lunch will be happy to provide you with some names." He glances at his watch. "Perfect timing. Let me take you to Keith's office."

Chapter 12

JULY 31, 1998

Lenny is on his way back to the airport from Moore-Plastics Inc., a client of Intelogic. It is late Friday afternoon and he has been driving for the last two hours. As usual, he refused to take a limousine. He likes to think while driving, it helps his concentration. And he has a lot to think about.

The direction of the solution, as pointed out by Scott, is still intact. They'll have to add something to their ERP system. Something that will cause their system to generate more value, bottom-line value, even for mid-range companies. But it's not an additional module that can be purchased; it is more involved than that. This was a hectic week, but he finally has it all figured out. Scott will be amazed. And pleased.

Lenny glances at his watch; he's making good time. In less than an hour he'll be on the plane and two hours later at home. But he doesn't feel like it. Since his divorce, and his wife getting custody of their daughter, Lenny's gotten used to being alone. As a matter of fact, he likes it. But not tonight. Not when he has so much to tell Scott, and the long weekend ahead of him.

He takes his cell phone and calls Scott. He gets Scott's voice mail. Not good enough. He dials Scott's private home line—a number only very few people at BGSoft have access to.

"Hello?" comes the voice of Scott's youngest child.

"Hi, Cindy, how are you darling? What's new with your virtual city? Did you add a lot to City2000?"

"Lenny," she sounds pleased. No wonder, kids love Uncle Lenny, especially those interested in the really clever computer games. "I added a university and you wouldn't believe how many people want to come to live in my city. There's no more land for buildings. What do you think, should I build another city not too far away?"

Lenny laughs. Cindy inherited her father's ambition; she always goes for more. "I'm sure you can. The question is whether that's the right thing to do. The investment might be very high. Have you thought about better exploiting the northeast part?"

Cindy would love to spend the next hour talking with Lenny, but her mother takes the phone. "Hi, Lenny. Are you all right? I expect Scott will be home around seven-thirty. Can he call you back?"

"Hi, Diane, how are you? I'd like to come over tonight and discuss some things with Scott. Do you mind?"

"On the contrary. Join us for dinner?"

"I'm afraid not. I'm landing too late, a little after eight. Thanks anyway."

"Don't thank me, just come. We'll wait with dinner. We're having a special dinner. I cooked it myself, so don't even think of eating any of that airline food."

Lenny groans at the thought of Diane's cooking, but he knows better than to argue with her. Besides, he'll get to spend time with the kids. "Thanks, Diane, see you soon."

Scott himself opens the door. He seems much more relaxed than the last time they met.

Smiling at Lenny, he says, "And here is the missing person, come in. I told them not to worry about you."

Lenny looks puzzled.

"You'd better find some good excuse for Roger and Mary-Lou," Scott warns him. "They've been trying to reach you for the last three days. Mary-Lou decided that you were kidnapped. What's the big idea, permanently shutting off your cell phone and not bothering to call in?"

Scott leads the way to the kitchen. "By the way, where have you been?"

"Working on something that you said was urgent and important. Do you want to hear?"

"After dinner." Diane kisses Lenny's cheek. "Kids! Dinner!"

It's after ten when Scott finally succeeds in pulling the kids off Lenny. They sit down by the pool, Lenny with a beer, Scott enjoying a Remy Martin. It's a lovely night, not too hot and with plenty of stars to stare at.

"Well," prompts Scott, "the last thing I heard was that you put three people to work calling a whole bunch of Intelogic's clients. Where have you been since then?"

"Do you want addresses or do you want to know what I found?"

Scott gestures with his glass, "Touché. Lay it on me in whatever way you want."

"Good. So, as you know, I started this week with a visit to Intelogic."

Scott, who for the past two days has been chased by a desperate Roger and then by a worried Mary-Lou, restrains himself from interrupting with "and then you disappeared into limbo."

Lenny, apparently unaware of the turmoil that he caused, continues. "I learned a lot. Mainly that Intelogic doesn't know why their software is bringing bottom-line benefits. Sorry, that's not quite accurate. The situation is much more grotesque. Their developers think that they know, then the sales people repeat development's claims like parrots, but none of them bother to see what actually happens with their own clients.

"Can you believe that they didn't ask themselves the most

basic questions? Like, what is the average return on investment their clients get with their software?"

"Lenny, why are you surprised? The same is true for us as well. Just a month ago we weren't making a connection between our product and the client's bottom line."

"But they're emphasizing bottom-line value," Lenny argues. "They should know better. Never mind. Let me continue. I met with their VP of sales, a funny guy. He doesn't know much about their product, but he tries to compensate with his jokes."

"You mean that he laughed at yours?"

"Come to think of it, he didn't tell me even one good joke. Anyhow, I told him that as part of the due diligence I wanted a list of all their clients. He wasn't surprised. Then I added that the list had to specify for each client the actual, or at least the expected, return on investment. He almost fell out of his chair." Lenny starts to giggle.

"I would've too," Scott says flatly.

Lenny smiles and continues. "Like anyone from sales, this funny guy is quick on his feet. He said he had prepared a list of their best references for me. Then he hands me the list. Eight customers! That's all. From the hundreds they've sold to? Of course I pressed him until I got the full list. I called the eight companies myself. And the long list I faxed back to the office to check."

"I've seen it," says Scott. "I also looked at the questions that you prepared for them."

"Only two simple questions." Lenny is proud of the first market survey he ever initiated. "How frequently do you run Intelogic? And, do you think you make more money from using the software? That's all. Have you seen the results of those calls?"

"No. I wanted to leave something for you to surprise me with."

"Good. I took the list of eight names and called them all. That was very enlightening. All eight claimed they use Intelogic and like it. Only five of them say they are making money by using the software. Out of these five only three have impressive results."

"What about the hundreds of phone calls that we made?"

"Didn't change the picture much. They produced another four companies who claim substantial results."

"So let me guess," Scott speculates, "the rest of the week you spent visiting all of them. Just like that. You don't know that those visits should have been scheduled weeks in advance?"

"Actually, that's just what the funny guy said. But ignorance is bliss," Lenny grins. "I asked him to call them, explain the purpose of my visit, and tell them the time I'd be arriving. There was no problem. All these plants are happy with Intelogic, and even happier to brag about their results. But I must admit that I dropped one. The plant in Malaysia. So I visited only six plants."

"In three days? Not bad considering the distances."

"Not bad at all. But let me tell you the more interesting parts. All six plants are using the software differently than Intelogic intended! Also, they all claim that it took them a significant amount of time to implement it—not because of technical problems, but because somehow they needed to achieve consensus on how to use it. Are you listening?"

Scott laughs. "Oh yes, I am. I'm not surprised though."

"You're not?" Lenny is puzzled. "Well, I was. I couldn't believe my ears. They actually told me, all six of them, that they had to re-think the entire way they run their operations. They had to change some of their most fundamental rules."

"Of course," says Scott smiling. "That's exactly what I expected."

This is too much for Lenny. "I don't see how you could expect it, unless you're psychic."

Scott pretends to smoke an imaginary pipe. "Elementary, my dear Watson. Just common sense and a good memory."

Lenny smiles. "So, once again, one of your famous analyses. Okay, let's hear it. But slowly please."

"Don't you want to finish telling me what you discovered?"

"No."

Scott swirls his cognac and takes a taste. "When does a new technology bring value?" he begins with a rhetorical question. "We expect that a new technology will bring benefits when, and only when, the new technology expands an existing limitation. It is simply common sense."

"Maybe to you. What do you mean?"

"If the new technology doesn't diminish any limitation whatsoever, there's no possible way in which it can create benefits. Do you agree with that?"

Lenny, searching for any crack in Scott's arguments, is not in a hurry to agree. But every example that he can think of validates Scott's argument.

Once Scott realizes that Lenny actually agrees, he continues. "At the same time, if something is a limitation, by definition it means that diminishing it brings a benefit. Otherwise it is not a limitation. That's why I claimed that a new technology will bring benefits, when, and only when, it surpasses an existing limitation. Can I continue?"

"Please do."

"Now let's establish the other pillar of my argument. It is also obvious that the mere fact that we are dealing with a new technology tells us that we have been living with an existing limitation for quite some time. Now ask yourself how we could live with this limitation. It must be that our customs, our habits, our measurements, our rules, recognize and consider the existence of that limitation."

"Now you have lost me."

"No, I didn't. But if you insist, I'll give you an example. Suppose that Mary-Lou gives me a letter to be signed, a letter that has to be sent to, let's say twenty people. And I find some major mistakes that I mark on the letter. Twenty years ago, when we still used typewriters and carbon copies, I would not have expected the letters to be sent out within the next hour. Not even by Mary-Lou.

"I would not have expected her to send the letters within the next hour, and I would not consider it as bad performance on her part. That is what I mean by my statement: our habits and measurements recognize and accommodate the existence of a given limitation."

When he sees that Lenny is still thinking, Scott adds, "The fact that our habits or rules accommodate the limitation should not be confused with us, as human beings, realizing that a limitation is actually a limitation." When he sees that his last comment hasn't helped to clarify things, he immediately explains. "For example, twenty years ago I didn't regard typewriters as a limitation. Not at all. As a matter of fact, if somebody had told me that a time would come when I myself would be able to make the corrections to the letter and have twenty copies in less than five minutes, I would have laughed in his face."

"I see," says Lenny. "Carry on."

"Now we install some new technology. Let's assume successful installation occurs; the limitation has been diminished. But what happens if as part of the implementation of this new technology we neglected to address the rules? What happens if we still operate with the old rules, the rules that assume the existence of the limitation?"

"In that case, the rules themselves will impose a limitation," Lenny says.

"Exactly. And then what benefits will we gain from the new technology?"

"I don't know," Lenny answers. "It depends on the technology and what it does. But I see your point. If we don't also change the rules we can be assured that we will not realize the full benefits."

Scott looks at the sky, still pretending to smoke his imaginary pipe. "You see, Watson, technology is a necessary condition, but it's not sufficient. To get the benefits at the time that we install the new technology, we must also change the rules that recognize the existence of the limitation. Common sense."

"Scott," Lenny says quietly. "You forgot one point. Without

changing the rules we are not going to get the full benefits, I grant you that. But maybe we are getting ninety-nine percent of the benefits? In that case, what you said is interesting, but immaterial."

He finishes his beer. "So, to convince me that new technology is not sufficient, you still have to show that without changing the rules we lose significant potential benefits. And I don't see how you can provide such proof." He stands up and walks into the house for another beer.

After two minutes Lenny is back, a frosty glass in his hand. "I found the real flaw in your arguments," he grins at Scott. "Who says we don't change the rules? Whenever we implement a new technology we change some rules. Take your example. Today you do expect that the letter will be corrected and sent almost immediately."

Scott is still relaxing on the lounge chair looking at the stars. "Do you remember when we had just started?" he reminisces. "We had a wonderful product, one of the first commercially available MRP packages. You wrote most of it yourself, and I sold more than half of the first fifty copies. It was new technology. Powerful new technology. And it was so much easier to explain than what we have now.

"The limitation that our package addressed was clear to all our prospects. Do you remember how difficult and time consuming it used to be to manually calculate the 'net requirement'? They had to take each order, and first determine what was already available in finished goods stock. Then they had to look at the making of the product, see what purchased components and materials were required, deduct from it what was already in process on the shop floor, and only then did they know what additional quantities had to be released to the shop.

"Remember how many people they needed for that work? In a plant of three hundred people they had at least twenty in material management. It was so much work that the rule was to do 'net requirement' only once a month. It was an unwritten rule, but it was the same rule in almost every plant. Do 'net requirement' only once a month. Even though it inflated the inventories. Even though it slowed the reaction time to new orders. There was no other way. For most plants, once a month was the practical maximum.

"And then we came up with our new technology, with the computer and our MRP package. And what took twenty people several days could all of a sudden be done overnight. What a technology. Do you remember?"

Lenny knows that Scott is setting him up. But the feeling of nostalgia is strong enough to cause him to sigh, "Of course I remember." In a harder tone he adds, "What's the point?"

"What's the point?" Scott says, still talking to the stars. "The point is that most of our customers were not so thrilled with the outcome. Yes, less manpower was needed to do the calculations, but more people were needed to maintain the data accurately on the computer. The disappointment was so large that our industry came up with the famous 'class A users,' the companies that were displayed as the model of how to do it right. Those companies that had taken the actions to maintain over ninety-eight percent data accuracy, that had done the 'proper' education on dependent and independent demand, on economical batch quantities and all that crap.

"Looking back, it was so ridiculous. Our customers didn't get enough benefits. Do you know why? Lenny, think. It was not because their data was not accurate enough, or because they didn't do enough technical education.

"You knew almost every one of our clients at that time. The ones that were constantly complaining about bugs and the few that were very happy with the results. The few happy ones that were reporting large reduction in inventories and substantial improvement in due-date performance. So tell me," Scott presses, "why so few got real benefits."

When Lenny doesn't reply, Scott provides the answer. "Because even with our system, most of our clients still ran 'net requirement' only once a month."

"You're right," Lenny bursts out laughing. "I can't believe it."

Scott summarizes. "Technology removed the limitation but the rule was left in place. Lenny, don't laugh. We were part of it. We didn't recognize it either. If we had, we could have sold many more systems. We were as blind as everyone else."

Lenny calms down. "How come nobody pays attention to the obvious?" he asks.

Scott doesn't have an answer. "I don't know," he says. "But the same is happening again with our new ERP technology. What is the limitation that our ERP system diminishes?"

"I would say that it provides much better visibility into operations," Lenny answers.

Scott smiles. "Lately, I've become allergic to that phrase. Let's say that the limitation that we diminish is the need to act without having all the information."

"Using our system the client has at his fingertips all the needed information," Lenny agrees, "no matter how big or diverse his operation is. We provide an enterprise-wide system."

Scott continues. "Our ERP technology substantially diminishes that limitation. But, what about the rules, the habits, the measurements?" After a short pause Scott answers his own question. "I suspect that many of the rules our clients currently use are still based on the old limitation. Take for example what we saw at Stein Industries. Maggie was impressed that they got rid of the local efficiencies. The rule that they have to strive to make every resource work all the time, regardless if what is produced is needed down the road. Let's face it, such a rule was probably necessary when they operated without having all the information. But now it is just preventing operations from getting the benefits."

"Well, as usual your analysis is right on the nose. Every place I visited that got bottom-line results also changed the rules. They don't attempt to reach high efficiencies on every work center. They don't behave as if releasing work orders early is the way to get early finish and they don't even think that the larger the batch, the better it is."

Scott is pleased. But there's another question that bothers him. "What did they replace those rules with?" Scott asks.

"What I've seen is that they replaced those rules with one form or another of Drum-Buffer-Rope," Lenny replies. "I don't mean just the mechanism, I mean the whole management approach. Some don't know the name, but still that's basically what they're doing."

"Something like what we saw at Stein Industries?"

"Basically, yes. More sophisticated. Less effective. No one is coming close to Gerry's performance, but then nobody is using a separate control system, a Buffer-Management approach."

"Why not?"

"Because Intelogic doesn't provide adequate time buffers."

"I want to understand. What you're telling me is that our crude MRP module with the change that you introduced for Gerry is working better than all those sophisticated APS systems? It's hard to believe." Scott is pleased but puzzled.

"Actually it is very simple once you hear the complaints about the fact that the schedules are unstable," Lenny explains. "Even if for a whole week they follow the schedule to the letter still the schedule they regenerate the next week is disjointed. Then you realize how important it is to confine the optimization to only the constraint. Doing more than that doesn't help. It hurts. It destabilizes the schedule.

"That's what Dr. Deming tried to teach us. That trying to optimize within the noise not only doesn't help, it hurts. As long as the system is vibrating within the limits of its noise, any tampering just increases the fluctuations."

Scott doesn't pretend to understand this statistical rule. Instead he concludes, "So we don't need to purchase an APS company, we . . ."

"I didn't say that," Lenny cuts him off. "We still need an APS."

"But why?"

"Because we need it to schedule the bottleneck," Lenny states.

"I thought that wasn't a big deal, that bottleneck scheduling can be done manually."

"It's not always as easy as in Gerry's plant." Seeing that Scott would like to hear more, he elaborates. "Take Irrigtech for example, one of Intelogic's customers that I visited. They have two complicating factors that made their life miserable. Their bottleneck is a work center with fifteen similar but not exactly identical machines. Their capabilities overlap, but they are different. Some can handle only small parts, some cannot process softer metals, et cetera, et cetera. The other factor is that most products go through the bottleneck work center more than once. This combination is pretty tricky to handle manually.

"Another kind of complication I've seen is even more difficult to handle manually. For example, take a company that deals with a special type of plastic. Imagine that in one work center you add the color. To move from producing one type of black parts to a different black part takes maybe five minutes; you just have to adjust some gadgets. But to move from producing black parts to producing white ones might take five hours. You have to almost disassemble the machine and clean it, otherwise instead of white parts you'll get gray. This is what they call 'dependent set-up times.'

"Of course they prefer to first produce all the parts of the same color before they move on to produce parts of another color. That's not the problem. In their case it gets really complicated because the work center that has to further process these parts also has 'dependent set-up time'. Unfortunately, this dependence is not due to color but due to another property like grain or width. So what we face are two work centers each having their own 'preferred sequence.' Now if you schedule according to the preferred sequence of the first work center, the second one will have to spend so much time doing set-ups that it will turn into a huge bottleneck. But if you schedule according to the second work center, the first one becomes a bottle-neck. You understand?"

"I just understand that you need a smart algorithm to help schedule the bottleneck," Scott says smoothly, "That's all I understand, but that's what I need to understand. So, Lenny, what are your recommendations?"

"Let's buy Intelogic and integrate it prudently into our MRP module. Making sure that only the bottlenecks will be optimized, that buffers will be inserted in the right places, and add a good Buffer-Management. It's not too big a deal."

"Do we really need Intelogic for that?"

"Yes. If we buy them I can dictate what part of their package to use within BGSoft. They are good developers. Once they see my analysis they will be able to deliver the code in a very short time. Look, with all the complicated scenarios I described before, it would take us months to program the algorithm. They already did that. We may use only twenty per cent of their existing code, but that alone is worth the price to us. And I can use their people. It's tough to get such capable people."

"Done," says Scott. "My next question is, who will help the clients to change the rules?"

"I don't know," Lenny answers. "But Scott, what I've learned this week is that Gerry is not such an exception. Many companies are already working according to the new rules. It makes sense. Many more want to do it but they cannot find a suitable system to support them. Besides, there are many consultants who are advocates of the Theory of Constraints, maybe we can use them?"

"So the real problem is us," Scott concludes.

"What do you mean?"

"Lenny, we'll have major problems with only our two arms handling the market. Gail and her people are so comfortable with selling technology that it will not be easy to convince them to switch to selling value."

"I've already noticed," Lenny agrees.

"And Maggie is no less of a challenge. She is terrified about going into anything that involves a culture change. And here, since we are talking about changing such fundamental rules, we are dealing with implementing a culture change. You see what I mean? The biggest obstacle is not the market or the product. It's us. How are we going to deal with it?"

"Thank God that's your problem." Lenny glances at his watch. "It's time to get some sleep. I'm dead tired."

Chapter 13

"You sure got all of that one, Craig," Maggie remarks. "Looks like that one went two-fifty."

Craig beams while dropping his driver back into his golf bag. "It was much better than that slice on the third hole. Never did figure out where that ball went."

"Those woods are pretty thick. I've been fortunate enough to search around in there myself."

Maggie was invited to Pierco's top executive retreat to give a half-hour presentation on the last stages of the ERP project. And, as every executive knows, there is no better opportunity for a golf game than an executive retreat.

It is an unusually beautiful day, brilliantly sunny and not a cloud in sight. The breeze off the ocean makes the temperature absolutely perfect for a friendly game of golf. Maggie and Craig are joined by two of Craig's division vice presidents, Brian and Stan.

"No, both of you go right ahead," Maggie motions to them. "I really don't mind hitting last. There's no good place to hide up by the women's tees anyway. Not that I don't trust you, of course."

"Of course," remark Brian and Stan in unison.

After each has hit a reasonable drive, they walk together to the women's tee. Maggie turns her attention to the task at hand, and with all of her concentration sends a beautiful 200-yard drive straight down the middle of the fairway.

"Not bad yourself," remarks Craig. "Looks like you out-drove Brian."

"The tee placement makes all the difference in the world." Maggie smiles sweetly.

"I just hate hitting over water," she continues as they walk down the fairway, caddies close behind. "Stan, I meant to ask you earlier. How are things going in your division now that the system has stabilized?"

After taking a long puff of his smelly cigar, Stan replies, "Honestly, I haven't seen that much of a difference."

"Now come on, Stan," says Craig. "Don't give Maggie such a hard time. I just told her that your divisional inventory is down thirty million dollars so far."

Stan shrugs and responds, "Yes, that's true, but you still can't make me believe that BGSoft was responsible for all that. We have done a lot of things to help reduce those inventories."

Maggie says with humor in her voice, "We all know that success has many parents, and that only a failure is an orphan."

Stan is a stocky man, a person you know to stay away from, unless you like to be the target of practical jokes. He was one of the few divisional managers who actively opposed the ERP project. Now that it was implemented and working well Maggie was hoping that he would have changed his mind. Well, some people never change.

With a straight face, he asks, "You want me to credit your system with something? Fine. I'll admit that it did make a difference."

"Let's hear it." Maggie is cautious.

"When I walk around," he says grinning, "there seem to be a whole lot more people sitting at computers, entering a whole lot more data."

Then he adds, "Not quite sure why we need it though. Whoever said that computers were going to eliminate paper should see our place. I think there's more paper than before."

"In ours too," Brian chimes in. "Last week during our division review, I told our director of Materials that the meaning of MRP hasn't changed with all the advancements in technology. The initials still stand for More Reams of Paper."

Stan is not going to let Brian steal his thunder. He waves his cigar and roars, "I told mine that MRP was More Ridiculous Priorities!" His laughter irritates her all the way to the green.

Stan takes one look and says, "Watch the break on that putt, Craig. Looks like it'll break right unless you power it in."

After missing the putt, Craig says dryly, "This time you were right, Stan. "Put me down for a bogie."

"That's a par for me," says Brian.

"Par for me, too," says Maggie.

"And I'm chirping like a birdie," adds Stan.

As they walk towards the next hole, Maggie starts again.

"Come on guys, I'm serious. The implementation went well and we all know you have good results. I would really like to get them written up as a case study."

"Depends on how you measure results," Stan retorts. "I agree that the system was installed on time and within budget. For the sake of argument, let's say that the system was responsible for the entire inventory reduction. But even with that, to me it caused more damage than benefits."

Maggie is unaware of any damage. She knows she doesn't have to ask. Since Stan is quick to air his gripes, she expects to hear the full details long before they reach the next hole. To her surprise Stan doesn't elaborate.

"What is the damage?" she finally asks.

"It's the predicted lift in sales," Craig answers.

She turns to look at him. "Actually, Maggie, it's me and my big mouth," he starts to explain. "One of the strongest arguments in the ERP justification was an expected increase in sales. Not only does it represent a substantial increase in our net profit, it was also so easy to show that it is clearly a result of implementing the system.

"For years we were unable to reduce shortages to less than

fifteen percent, and now, in just six short months, we got down to less than ten. Nobody can claim that it was a fluke, or because of other things we did. Not even our friend Stan here."

Stan exhales a puff of heavy smoke. Craig pats him on the back and continues. "Since everybody knows that fewer shortages mean more sales, I had a clear case. No wonder that in the board meeting I shoved it down the weasel's throat."

"I would have loved to be there." Maggie can't help laughing. "Seeing that troublemaker's face . . ." Then she notices that the others are not laughing."

"That was a mistake," Craig sighs, "a big mistake."

Stan mutters something unclear through his nose.

Seeing Maggie's surprise, Brian volunteers an explanation.

"Well," he says, "that new board member isn't just a weasel, he's a real sly fox. Since Craig was so confident about the sales lift, this no-good punk wanted to know how come we hadn't updated the sales forecast for the rest of the year. To save face we had to do it, and now we're stuck."

Maggie has to check. "From your gloomy faces I gather that there was no increase in sales?"

"Of course not," Stan barks. "Do you know how many factors impact the level of sales? Trillions!"

Seeing the nasty look Craig is sending him, he raises his cigar. "Okay, I exaggerated, not a trillion, just a few dozen. Two percent increase, bah! Anything can wash out a change that small. The market becomes softer, the competitor reduces his price, you name it. And yes, Maggie, before you ask, last quarter my sales stayed as flat as Kansas."

Maggie looks at Brian.

"Sorry, Maggie, it's even worse in my division. Inventory went down, shortages went down, but sales have gone down too. Over four percent."

"Maggie, gentlemen, I think we are holding up the next foursome," says Craig.

Maggie watches where Craig hits, and lines up her tee shot to be in the same area.

"Tough break you two," Stan quips. "It's going to be hard to get on the green from there."

"Yeah, yeah," Craig responds, and then turns to Maggie. "Ready to walk?"

"You bet!" Maggie replies.

"Craig, I'm really glad that you arranged this golf game," Maggie teases. "And I thought you just wanted to 'get out for some fresh air.' Isn't that what you said?"

"Well, I know you pretty well." Craig smiles. "I was confident you would ask about results in Brian's and Stan's divisions before we reached the fifth hole."

"Have I become that predictable?" Maggie asks softly.

"There's more than one reason why we like working with KPI Solutions. But the most important one is that when you sell a job, you see it through—not like some of your competitors," Craig explains. "After your team did such a thorough job on the bottom-line analysis for my board, I knew you would follow up on it."

"Explanation accepted." Maggie is back in a good mood.

"Maggie, the reality is that the results we extrapolated from the first division have not materialized in these two divisions."

"Craig, what do you want me to do? The system works fine, shortages are down. And as Stan said, there are many outside reasons for sales not going up."

"Correct, but the situation is more involved than that. Brian is desperate, and he might put me, and also you, in an uncomfortable situation. Maybe you can do something about it. Have a chat with him."

They keep walking silently. Maggie is uncomfortable. She doesn't understand how she found herself in this awkward situation. This weekend was supposed to be fun. But now it looked like they were blaming her for something KPI had nothing to do with.

"That sounds about right," Maggie says to her caddie when he suggests a four iron.

It's amazing how they figure out what club length you need

so quickly, she thinks. Listening to the caddie on a new course can make a world of difference. They know how to approach the hole and what traps to avoid. Always listen to an expert. Then, remembering some less pleasant experiences, she thinks, watch out for a rookie pretending to be an expert.

That was my mistake, she realizes. I'm a rookie pretending to be an expert. Why did I offer to do that bottom-line justification for Craig?

KPI is a company of system integrators. We're good at it. The best. But we are not management consultants. Why did I stick my nose into something that KPI doesn't have any expertise in? Craig could have done it himself and KPI would have been okay. Nobody would have blamed us for something we didn't have anything to do with. But no, I had to go and do this stupid justification, and now look where I am.

Maggie, she promises herself, from now on stick to what you are good at, never again pretend to be someone you are not. She feels much better.

"Watch that chip up, Stan," Brian calls out. "There's a nasty slope on that green."

All four putt out. "Looks like that hole goes to Maggie," Stan says. "So far Craig has the lead with two holes, but it is still anyone's game. That steak is going to taste even better when you pick up the tab, Brian."

"Don't get too confident," retorts Brian. "The game is still young."

While waiting to tee off at the next hole, Brian turns to Maggie. "I want to talk to you."

Seeing her reluctant expression, he immediately adds, "Maggie, I'm sorry that we gave you the impression that we blame BGSoft. Well, maybe because of what happened we committed ourselves to the board for something we shouldn't have. And I can't say that I'm happy with the situation. But Maggie, you don't have to tell me that my drop in sales is not connected, in any way, to your work. I know exactly why my sales dropped."

"Why?" Maggie's natural curiosity forces her to ask.

"Two months ago we launched a major upgrade to one of our product lines," Brian answers. "It's quite an important line, about a quarter of our business. The new products are great; a substantial improvement over what we offered before. Of course, the minute we started advertising, the demand for the 'old' products dropped sharply, but the problem is that we can't produce enough of the new products."

"I told you not to annouce that product line so early," Stan interjects. "My philosophy is to first stock the warehouse with enough inventory, then announce your product. Everybody knows you can't sell from an empty wagon."

Craig chides, "Yes Stan, we all know your philosophy on inventory. That's probably why you had the largest reduction—your division had the most to start with."

Maggie chooses to continue talking to Brian. "So, now you're busy increasing the plant capacity; buying more machines and hiring more people. Do you think you can gear up fast enough to have sufficient sales before the end of the year?"

"Not at the rate we're moving now. That's why I wanted to talk to you."

KPI is a system integrator, she reminds herself. That helps to overcome her instinctive tendency to always look for opportunities. "I don't see how we can help," she says flatly.

"Maybe you can," Brian insists. "Let me explain to you what I really want. My division doesn't have the budget this year to buy machines or to hire more people."

"I decided," Craig says, "that for Pierco, it is less damaging if Brian's division misses their sales forecast than if they overrun the budget by so much."

"Which leaves me only one alternative," Brian continues. "I must optimize the use of the capacity I do have. In other words, I want to install an advanced planning and scheduling system. And I need to do it fast. From what I'm told, it can give me the additional twenty percent I need. Can you help us install such a system?"

"I don't like it," Craig steps in. "One of the main reasons for moving to an ERP system was to get rid of all the local systems; to have uniformity across the board. And now, before we've even finished rolling out BGSoft, we're already starting to put in 'private' systems? How will it look to the board?"

Before anybody can comment, he adds, "I know that BGSoft doesn't offer an APS as part of their system. But I read they have just purchased Intelogic. Is it already integrated? We're willing to be a beta test."

Brian doesn't look happy about being a guinea pig, but he doesn't object. It is clear to Maggie that they've discussed this before.

"We're up," Stan says. "C'mon—are you going to hit or talk?"

"We're hitting," Brian calls back. "Keep your pants on."

The opportunity for new business is clear, but Maggie is also aware of the pitfalls. She decides to move cautiously. There is no point in taking a system integration job and then falling flat on your face because of management issues.

When they walk to the green Maggie makes sure that Craig is in hearing distance and then asks, "Brian, do you know what it takes to achieve real results with an APS system?"

When Brian doesn't answer, she continues, "Are you aware that some fundamental rules will have to be changed? For example, do you know that you will not be able to continue judging the plants by their efficiencies?"

"What do you mean?" Craig sounds surprised. "The whole idea is to increase efficiencies."

Brian steps in, "Don't worry, Craig. I'm not planning to hire more people and I do intend to produce more with the same people. I'll even reduce the inventories at the same time. So what do you care if the efficiency numbers go down?"

"If you can do all that, I don't care."

"I think that it's just a lot of baloney," Stan declares. "But, as always, Brian is latching on to the newest fad. Good luck Brian, and don't forget what I'm telling you, falling for those fads is a recipe for breaking a leg."

Maggie can't stand people who laugh loudly at their own jokes.

Brian also ignores him. Turning back to Maggie he says, "Other system integrators see the implementation of an APS as if it is just another system implementation. I see that you understand the real difficulties. That's great."

So, he has already checked with the competition. Before asking KPI. Never mind, that will shorten the time to get a contract from him, Maggie thinks to herself. But she is not yet ready to offer her services. She invested too much in Pierco to risk it all by carelessly jumping into uncharted waters.

"Brian, I have to know about these things, that's my profession. But how come you know so much?"

"Because my comptroller is crazy about the Theory of Constraints. He went to a workshop on it and for the last six months that's all he talks about. And he can talk a lot."

Maggie and Brian continue to talk throughout the rest of the round.

After everyone putts on the eighteenth green, Stan says, "Looks like that one is yours too, Craig. It looks to me like you won the game as well. Nice round."

As they walk up to the clubhouse, Stan bellows, "What is everyone drinking? This round's on me."

Over drinks Brian asks, "Maggie, what do you think, can you help me?"

"Brian," Maggie says, "let me ask you one more question. What do you really want to implement in your plants, a sophisticated optimizer or a good Drum-Buffer-Rope system?"

"I want results. Fast results. There are only three months left till the end of the year, and I am considerably behind."

"The objective is clear. Now let's talk about the obstacles. We agreed that education plays a vital role in such an implementation."

Craig interrupts, "I'm all for education, but keep in mind that Brian doesn't have any time to spare. Can't he do the education at a later stage?"

"No, Craig," Brian answers. "This is a totally different ball game. How can I explain it clearly? Well, let me put it this way. You know that we need about twenty percent more capacity. One way is to stay with convention and buy more machines for thirty-eight million dollars, and hire an additional two hundred people. You won't allow me to do it. That's fine, because even if you approve the expenditure I will not be able to put the machines in place to affect this year's results.

"So what we're trying here is the other way. The idea is to abolish the traditional way of running a plant in order to gain, within a few weeks, the twenty-percent capacity that we badly need. We are not only going to change the traditional rules, we are also going to change the measurements. Maggie mentioned efficiencies. That's one of them. I don't have to tell you how careful we have to be about changing the measurements."

"You're going to do that?" Stan is surprised.

"Yes, I am. I may be crazy, but I'm not a fool. I can put whatever system I want on the computer. That's not the problem. But if I want to see results I have to do much more. It will succeed only if everyone in the plants, from the plant manager to the machinist, understands why we're making these changes. And why it makes perfect sense to do it. That's the education that Maggie is talking about. That step must be accomplished before any schedule generated by the computer hits the floor."

Craig shows that he understands and agrees.

"As I told you," Maggie starts again, "KPI is not a management consulting company. We are not the ones to do the educating. So who will?"

"My people," Brian answers confidently. "They're been preparing themselves for it for months. If they sold me on the idea, they can sell anybody. Don't worry, Maggie, that front is covered. What about the software? What's the story with the Intelogic deal? Is Intelogic already integrated into the main system?"

Maggie makes up her mind. If she doesn't grab this opportunity, Scott and Lenny would never forgive her.

"Not exactly. What BGSoft has done is to strip the over-so-phisticated features from Intelogic and place it as an integral part of the scheduling module. It's not going to be offered as an optimizer but as a powerful Drum-Buffer-Rope system."

"Exactly what we need!" Brian exclaims.

"And on top of that they're adding a comprehensive Buffer-management system."

"Perfect," Brian whispers.

"The only problem is that is hasn't been tested outside the laboratory walls. But the first one to be a beta test will get Lenny's full attention. You know Lenny, right?"

"When do you think we can start?" Brian asks eagerly.

"You want to meet this year's sales forecast? We'd better start on Monday. We must make sure that everything is up and running before the end of this month."

"That's the spirit," Brian replies.

"Wait, wait," Stan waves his cigar, "I want to understand what's happening here. Brian, are you serious? Do you think that with shuffling something in the plants and putting in some fancy system you can get a twenty percent increase in capacity? I don't believe it. Have you been smoking something?"

"Stan, I intend to meet my sales forecast without spending a fortune on new machines or new people. You're going to be eating my dust."

"Fat chance. Tell you what, if you pull off a miracle of those proportions I'll eat my hat. No, even better, I'll invite Maggie to implement it in my division."

Craig laughs. "It's easier to believe that Brian will meet his forecast than that you'll invite computers in." More seriously he asks Maggie, "Your standard terms, and you'll put as many experienced people as we need on the project?"

"Absolutely."

"Brian, I think you can shake hands with Maggie. We have a deal."

Chapter 14

DECEMBER 28, 1998

They are all gathered in Scott's office. It's the end of the year, and on the surface, it's the best year in BGSoft's history. In spite of tightening conditions they not only succeeded in maintaining their rate of growth, they substantially increased their annual profits.

But Scott's frightening predictions are coming true. The ERP industry as a whole is now under the gun. A month ago, one of their main competitors forecasted negative growth for the quarter. Just before Christmas another announced that they were going to lay off six hundred people. The investment community is shocked. Of course the shares of these two ERP companies have plummeted, and are now trading at twenty percent of last month's value.

The investors are looking for an answer to the real question: what is the future of the ERP industry? Is what they see just the separation of the wheat from the chaff, the emergence of the true leaders? Or has the industry reached its growth limits? The answer is extremely important. If the first answer is right, then the companies still leading are the hottest bets around. But if the second alternative is true, then the faster the shares are dumped the better.

"Well, my dear friends," Scott starts the meeting, "our shares are still holding up, but last week was just the prelude. Next week is our real test. We'll have to give a lot of answers to a lot of prudent people. The situation, as you are well aware, is extremely sensitive. So we'd better make sure that we are all radiating exactly the same, clear message. Any hesitation on our part, any discrepancy, and we'll be drawn and quartered."

"Do we have a clear message to radiate?" Lenny asks.

"The problem is not the clarity of the message, but which message we choose to radiate," Scott answers confidently. "There are two alternatives and we have to choose one. This is probably the most important decision we have ever had to make."

All three quietly wait for him to continue.

"We are now at a crossroads," Scott explains. "We always knew that the time would come when we would be unable to continue growing at the phenomenal rate we've maintained for the last five years. The question is, are we going to decide that it's time to slow down, or do we have what it takes to keep going?"

Gail is uncomfortable. "Scott, you talk as if it's our decision, as if it isn't dictated by the objective conditions of our markets."

"Yes," Scott replies. "I'm convinced that it is in our hands. We can decide to continue doing business as we have always done. In that case we'd better admit that we are quickly reaching the saturation of our main and most lucrative market.

"Or we can decide to change the way we do business. It is risky, very risky. But, if we have the vision, the courage, and the determination to institute such a change, then in my opinion, the market is practically unlimited. Then, what we have achieved so far is nothing compared to what is waiting around the corner."

None of them says a word. They still wait for him to continue.

"If we choose the first alternative, then my advice is to tell the story as it is. There is no point in trying to persuade the analysts that we can sustain a forty percent rate of growth for long, when we can't do it, not for more than two or three quarters. Now is the best time to lower expectations."

"Can we do that without hurting our reputation?" Maggie asks.

"Yes," Scott answers. "We'll explain to the analysts the facts of life in our industry, the fact that the only real market is the large companies, and that in this market the ERP industry has reached saturation. If we do a good enough job we won't lose our reputation, and therefore should feel no negative impact on our market share.

"We are a solid company with a large customer base, with no debts to speak of and plenty of cash in the bank. The company's survival is not in question. Yes, our share value will dive, but after a time the market will stabilize. I think that the shares will level off at about a third of where they are now. But we all knew what would happen once we reached maturity."

Scott stops, waiting for the others to comment.

After a long silence, Gail starts to talk slowly, sharing her thoughts with the others. "This is strange. I always thought that it would be nice to slow the pace, to live without the constant pressure of meeting the next quarter's forecast. But now, when for the first time this option becomes real, I feel the opposite."

Almost apologetically she adds, "I don't know about you guys, but I don't think I can enjoy life without constant pressure. After so many years, I think I've become addicted to it."

"I don't have the option of relaxing," Maggie comments. "The relationship between our companies is such that even if BGSoft slows down to zero growth, KPI will still have to expand for the next couple of years. But Gail," Maggie smiles sympathetically, "I understand exactly what you mean. We're too young to slow down."

"Scott," Lenny says, "we heard one very unattractive option. What's the other?"

"The other alternative is to convince the analysts that we are a company with tremendous future potential. In the current state of affairs, I'm afraid that it's not sufficient to promise that we can maintain our traditional growth. To insure that the analysts will not ignore our explanation as just not air we have to up the stakes. If we want to convince them that we will continue to be the dominant player, we have to declare that our target is to grow at a rate of at least sixty percent—and then convince them that it is doable."

"But that's impossible!" Gail exclaims.

"If you believe that it's impossible, then it is impossible," Scott replies flatly. "Then we're back to the first alternative."

"But Scott, be reasonable," Gail pleads. "It will not be easy to make five hundred million a quarter, and you're talking about promising much more than that."

"Yes, Gail. That is exactly what I'm saying. We cannot do it if we continue to do business as we have always done. If we elect to go the growth path we must institute an entirely different strategy and tactics. We have to change."

"To what?" Gail snaps.

Scott answers decisively. "We have to switch from selling information technology to selling value."

Scott's answer is not a surprise to Gail. For the last three months it's been floating in the air. So far she has been unwilling to even consider it. Now she realizes that there is something she hates even more. Stagnation. Still, she doesn't like it, not at all.

"Selling value is a nice phrase," Gail says flatly. "But can you tell me what it really boils down to?"

"We've just started understanding what it's really all about," Scott answers. "At this stage, we only know where to start and where to look for more answers." Then he adds, "I wish we had more time to explore things, but as it stands we have to make our decision now. Still my intuition tells me that concentrating on value will enable us to grow BGSoft to at least tenfold the size it is now."

It is Gail's responsibility to bring in the sales, and for that she needs much more than just a gut feeling. "Where do you suggest we start? And why do you think it will bring in the numbers we need?" she asks.

"In the last quarter we established a solid beachhead," Scott replies. "I hope that it's enough for a good start. Maggie, can you brief us on the latest developments in Pierco? In detail, please."

"Let me first stress," Maggie says, "that the implementation at Pierco was done under ideal conditions. We cannot expect as wonderful a setting in other places. As you know, it was done under the blessing of the CEO, and the divisional VP saw it as the only thing that could save his ass. It was led by the plant managers who personally supervised the education. And it was done under real pressure to achieve results in a very short time; they had to get enough increase in sales before the end of the year."

Lenny remarks jokingly, "Nothing focuses people's attention more than the realization that they are going to be hung the next morning."

"You can say that again," Maggie smiles. "Everybody collaborated, the resistance was minimal. Actually, I didn't see resistance at all. What about you, Lenny? You visited them at least once a week."

"I didn't see any resistance," he confirms. "On the contrary, my impression is that everybody was enthusiastic. I think that they did an excellent job bringing everybody on board."

"Did you start in all the plants at the same time?" Gail asks.

"No," Maggie answers. "We started with the two plants producing a new product line, plants that did not have enough capacity."

"How much time did it take you to install our new MRP module?"

"That was beautiful. They understood exactly what they

wanted from our system. And we were not distracted by demands to force the system to do what their old systems used to do. It's hard to believe, but we were generating schedules two weeks after we started, and those schedules were followed from day one. Lenny, I think that you struggled a bit with the Buffer management, but even that was up and running a week later."

Lenny comments. "We needed to do quite a few additions, they had many things that we hadn't taken into account when we wrote the code. But it wasn't a big deal. Actually it was a delight. It's been a long time since I've worked on something that made perfect sense. We didn't have to complicate the system just to accommodate some irrational demands. In every case it was obvious to everybody what should be done. I think that the fact that everything was geared to one thing, achieving real results, gave everybody this rare clarity."

"I agree," Maggie says. "In all the years I've been implementing systems I've never seen such a focused, speedy implementation."

"Why are you surprised?" Gail asks. "Correct me if I'm wrong, but BGSoft was installed there before you started with this effort. So it wasn't a real implementation, it was just polishing what was already there."

"No, Gail," Maggie corrects her. "As you know, we usually start our ERP implementation with the financial modules, and the last thing installed is the MRP. In these plants, in fact in most Pierco plants, we hadn't even started the MRP implementation. And you know how much time it takes to install. In spite of all the promises that the data is accurate, it never is, and it's a long and tedious hassle to clean it up."

"So what was different? How did you manage a full, live implementation in just two weeks?"

Maggie smiles. "I have to agree with Lenny. When everything is focused toward results it is totally different from what we are used to. Having accurate data on the computer is not a target. Results are. The beauty of the Drum-Buffer-Rope is that it focuses your efforts. It tells you what the one percent is that's really important, and what's just niceties."

Realizing that Gail cannot possibly understand, Maggie elaborates. "They told us where the bottlenecks are, and together we cleaned the data up to the point that the system reached the same conclusion. Nothing more. It took less than two days. We left all the rest of the data as is and we went live on the floor. Surprise, surprise, it was good enough. Once Buffer management was up and running, all other meaningful mistakes got highlighted and then we corrected them."

"What are the results?" Scott asks.

Maggie beams. "Better than anyone hoped for. Brian, the VP in charge of the division where we did it all, was wrong about one thing. He underestimated how much the market is eager to buy his new product line. He thought that he needed twenty percent more capacity to satisfy the market demand. Well, in November we produced thirty-five percent more than in September, and we were still barely coping with the market pull. Needless to say, he is very happy. We moved fast enough to enable him to exceed the sales forecast for the year, so now he's a hero."

Gail is still trying to process this information. "Maggie, you are saying that our system provided thirty-five percent more capacity? Just like that?"

Maggie answers cheerfully. "It's even better than that. December daily rates are better than November and we haven't yet seen the full impact. You see, Gail, there's another factor that we didn't think about when we started. And that is LEAN."

"You mean the method that combines TQM and JIT?" Gail is surprised. "I don't know much about it but it was my understanding that LEAN aims at reducing waste, at eliminating non-value-added activities?"

"Well," Maggie answers, "under Buffer management, it's doing much more. All LEAN initiatives are now directed by the information that is generated by Buffer management. So in

Brian's plants they don't waste any effort dealing with vague concepts like non-value-added activities. In his plants LEAN is now focused on increasing capacity and increasing the flow. It's amazing how much capability is unearthed every week."

"Does Brian plan to spread Drum-Buffer-Rope and Buffer management to the other five plants in his division?" Scott asks.

"Already done," Lenny answers. "A week before Christmas we provided the features that were needed for the last plant."

"All seven plants are up and running," Maggie assures him. "And listen to this. Next week I'm going with Brian to Stan's division. We have an entire morning with all the plant managers. Also, Craig wants us to do the same for every plant in Pierco—all thirty-two of them. This thing turned out to be much bigger than I originally thought."

"Good for you," Gail says.

"It's also good for us," Lenny comments.

"Of course."

Deducing from Gail's tone of voice that she is probably unaware of the real impact it has on BGSoft, Lenny says, "There's something else that's important for you to know," he stresses. "This implementation in the plants has a major positive side effect on us."

"Besides our reputation, you mean?"

"Yes. Did your account manager have a chance to update you on the concurrent users in these plants?" Lenny asks.

Gail looks at Maggie.

Maggie explains. "Traditionally the plants have not been a good source of concurrent users for you. As you know, in a plant of a thousand people you rarely have more than twenty concurrent users. Well, with Buffer management the picture is very different. Every single foreman and everyone in the service department is now intensively using our system. In Brian's division, and I'm talking about all seven plants, the number of concurrent users is over six hundred. I believe that yesterday

George notified your account manager to invoice Pierco in accordance."

"Yahoo!" Gail squeals.

"Yes, I knew you'd be happy to hear about it," Lenny says. "It does change the picture, doesn't it?"

Gail nods. "It certainly does. Maggie, do you think that such a jump will happen in any plant that uses Buffer management, or is it unique to Pierco?"

"I don't think it's unique. Lenny, you understand the system much better than anybody else. What do you think?"

"It's generic," he says flatly.

"Well, my friends," Scott says, "what can we deduce from the Pierco experience? Gail?"

"I still have to digest what I've just heard," she answers. "But if our new addition really has such an impact on the number of concurrent users, it's very good news."

Scott is still looking at her, so Gail elaborates. "As you know, I've always claimed that there is still a very large market within our present group of customers. Many BGSoft clients have a relatively low number of concurrent users.

"In industrial companies the largest department, in terms of people, is production—often production comprises more than half of the total employees. Until now that has always been the department with the least number of users. We are very strong in finance, in sales, and even purchasing, but never in production. Now, if what I'm hearing is true, we can use it to bring in much more income. Considering our large, existing customer base, the potential here is big."

"That's what I thought," Scott confirms.

For the first time Gail sees this vague concept of selling value translated into something meaningful, very meaningful. She is forced to rethink her position.

While she is still trying to assimilate, Scott continues. "Maggie, do you have anything to add?"

"Not at this stage."

"Maggie," Scott tries again, "we are now facing a new situation. The reputations of two of our major competitors have been severely damaged. Their names are smeared in the newspapers and all the business magazines. That can't possibly give their customers a sense of security.

"Now we also know that ERP's strong side is not in the plants, and that the production modules, like the MRP, are usually the last to be implemented." He stops.

Maggie sees clearly where Scott is heading. "And you think that we now have something extraordinary to offer them."

"Don't we? Maggie, you've performed miracles in Brian's plants. How long did it take to reach tangible results? Six weeks? Eight?"

"Less than that. But Scott, that was a unique case. We didn't have to persuade them to change the rules, they did it themselves. We didn't have to do the really difficult part, the education. They did it themselves."

To Scott's surprise, Gail addresses Maggie's concerns.

"Since Lenny reappeared from his Intelogic week, I have done a market survey," Gail says.

She didn't like the fact that Lenny had initiated his survey on Intelogic customers, using her people, without having the decency to even inform her. Knowing that there was no point discussing it with Lenny, as he wouldn't even understand what she was complaining about, she moved to block any future intrusion on her territory. Sensing that Lenny and Scott would soon want to know more about the extent to which TOC is known and spread, she initiated a survey. Now she can share the information with them.

"Maggie, the market, and I'm also talking about plants of large companies, is ready for our new product. And there are many excellent consultants with good reputations who are advocates of TOC. Almost zealots, I should say. I've assembled a long list of them."

Lenny comments, "I'm not surprised. The logic of TOC is addictive. It's so refreshing to finally find something that's comprehensive, practical and still common sense."

Maggie leans forward, nodding in agreement. "After the Pierco implementation I know exactly what you mean. To answer your question Scott, considering what we've just heard, I think you're right. If a significant portion of the market is already using TOC, then there is a tremendous opportunity for us to do more business. We should target the production plants of the clients of our less fortunate competitors. I have no intention of promising results within four weeks. But if they buy the concept and are committing up front to do the education, I will not hesitate to guarantee results within less than three months. That should be enough."

"If you promise to deliver such fabulous results within three months, that's more than enough," Gail tells her. "We have a good chance of quickly penetrating many of their clients. Once in, we can spread out to replace the entire system." She quickly runs the numbers in her mind. "That's an even bigger opportunity than capturing more concurrent users within our own clients." Gail is becoming enthused.

Maggie nods in agreement and Gail continues. "So we have to team up with the TOC consultants and work out a joint presentation. Their job will be to sell the concept, ours to sell the software. Maggie, do you see any problem here?"

"Looks like a win-win to me," Maggie confidently answers.

Scott smiles. He is pleased. However, he knows that what they have discussed so far is not enough for the long run. He wants to make sure that they all see the big picture.

"We've discussed the opportunities open for us now in production," he says, "but in addition to production, there are two large sectors of our clients to whom we have offered, so far, very little. I'm referring to the engineering and Information Technology departments. In many companies these two sections combined are as large as production, if not larger."

Lenny bursts out laughing.

"Isn't it funny?" he says, still laughing loudly. Seeing the others' surprised looks he calms himself and explains, "For years we've been dealing with IT people. They're our main contacts. Still, what help do we offer them with their daily work? Nothing. Don't you think that's funny?"

"What do you mean by helping with their daily work?" Gail is slightly irritated.

Scott interjects in his calm voice, "Both Information Technology and engineering are quite different from the other functions in an organization. They deal with projects. And not just one project at a time. Almost each person is involved with multiple projects. We've found out how to help production, think what will happen if we can help these multi-project sections. If we can help them finish their projects on time, within budget, and without compromising on the content, think how much more we can offer our clients."

"Is it feasible?" Gail is all business.

"I think so," Scott answers. "We used a TOC solution for production, and there's a comparable application for multi-project environments. In the last month I've read everything I could put my hands on. The logic seems impeccable. If it works even half as well as the production solution, it's of tremendous value. As a matter of fact, I want to test it here, in BGSoft. What do you think Lenny?"

"We can sure use help in our programming projects," Lenny doesn't hesitate to announce. "And Scott, I wanted to surprise you, but since you happened on it, we are already testing in our Santa Cruz development center and in our center in India. In each case we're testing on a cluster of several projects."

"When did you write the software?" Scott is surprised.

Lenny smiles. "I didn't. And in Santa Cruz we're using a different software than in India."

"There are already commercially available packages?" Scott concludes more than asks.

"Yes. Very new and provided by very small companies. I've already checked." Lenny is pleased with himself. "We can buy them for a song. And to answer your unspoken question, Scott, so far it looks good; all early indications show that the theory does work."

Scott takes this aspect almost for granted. He moves on. "When do you think we can be ready with a multi-project module fully integrated into our ERP?"

"Third quarter next year shouldn't be a problem."

"Gail," Scott smiles, "what do you think about having such a product? It will open huge, new markets—the construction industry, software vendors—not to mention industries like banking and insurance, with so many projects."

"It opens interesting possibilities." Gail is still hesitant.

Scott doesn't press the issue. "You beat me to it," he congratulates Lenny.

"For a change." Lenny smiles back.

Scott lets the mood settle and then asks, "What are we going to say to the analysts? 'Gloom and doom' or the 'we just started' alternative?"

None of the three says a word, they just nod and share a small smile.

"We need a good presentation for the analysts," Scott reminds them. "And we need it for the second of January. That gives us less than three days, assuming you don't want to work on New Year's."

"We sure don't," Gail agrees. Knowing that she will be the one to prepare the presentation she pushes on. "How do you think we should start the presentation?"

Scott doesn't have any difficulty answering. "I suggest we begin by trying to convince the analysts that the only real market for our industry is the large companies. We show them that conventional ERP is of tremendous value for large companies and not such a great deal for mid-sized companies. I don't think that they understand this. We didn't."

Gail understands quickly. "We'll give statistics about the time, effort and resulting income for a sale to a mid-sized company as compared to a large company. Then we can present data on the current ERP penetration into the large-size market."

"What's the point starting like that? Why don't we begin with what we are planning to do permanently?" Maggie asks.

Scott answers. "We have to start with a good explanation of the problem. That will guarantee that our competitors will not be able to pretend that business is going as usual. If the problem is understood, our competitors will be forced to come up with solid answers on how they are going to continue to expand. I believe that at the moment, we are the only one with answers. If the analysts buy it, they will flag us as the clear leader."

"Besides," Gail contributes, "presenting them with a solid analysis of what's really going on gains their trust."

"Once this stage is reached," Scott continues, "they will probably ask about our plans. Then we'll present our strategy, enlarging within existing clients and expanding to competitors' clients. But if we just explain the strategy without backing it up by facts, they will ignore it as wishful thinking and we are doomed."

Gail picks up the baton. "We'll show them that we're actually prepared to do it. That it's not just empty words. I suggest that before we present our new modules we show what these modules can do. We show them the results actually achieved in Pierco. That will knock their socks off. Maggie, can you check with Craig and get his permission? I would like to use Pierco's name."

"No problem. He owes us so much, I don't think he will object. I suspect he might be willing to personally talk to the analysts."

"That would be superb," Scott remarks. "Gail, can you prepare some numbers? How many more concurrent users do we expect to get in our client base, how many in our competitors' clients? Broken down by country, quarter and so on?"

"No problem," Gail says. "What do you want the final number to be?"

"Gail, whatever we say next week to the analysts, we'll have to deliver. So what's the highest we can commit to?"

Gail immediately responds, "Can I answer after I do some checking? Maggie, I need your help here."

"We can work on it today," Maggie answers. "And if necessary, I'll clear tomorrow as well."

"Thanks. Scott you'll get our answer no later than tomorrow night."

Scott nods. "It's important to show the analysts that we don't put all our eggs in the production basket." He turns to Lenny. "We'll need a great presentation about our multi-project offer. We need to prove that we can take the entire market. I'll prepare the numbers to give a good indication of the size of that market. Lenny can you prepare the presentation?"

"Consider it done."

Five minutes after they all leave, Lenny is back again. "Scott, we forgot to talk about the most important direction. What about the mid-range market?"

"What do you think we should do about it?"

"What do you mean, 'what should we do about it'?" Lenny is excited. "We should charge! We have a product that brings value. What are we waiting for?"

Scott stays calm. "Charge? With what troops?"

"You mean, we can't tell Gail what to do?" Lenny is disgusted.

"That's not the issue. What we have just put on the table will absorb the time of every person she has for the next year."

Lenny doesn't buy it. "We can start a marketing campaign now and hire more people. With the other companies shaking, it will not be expensive to grab their best people."

"Lenny, if it was just a problem of manpower then you would be right. But it's more a problem of management attention. It is dangerous to charge in too many new directions at once. Besides, don't you see that we're not yet ready to approach the mid-market?"

Lenny sits down. After a long silence, he asks, "Why aren't we ready?"

"Lenny, so far we've succeeded in providing value only for production. What about the other functions? Don't you see that going with what we have now into the mid-market puts us on the same level as the APS companies? This might hurt our image—our image as an ERP company, as a provider of enterprise-wide systems. We invested so much effort to build this image, should we ruin it now?"

Lenny thinks about it. "I see your point. Right now we have one module that brings value. Once we're ready with the multi-project, we'll have two. I agree that to preserve our image as a quality provider of enterprise-wide systems we need much more than that. Scott, when do you think we'll be ready? Will we ever be?"

"It will take time, but I'm sure we will be able to come up with a new, and great value-driven enterprise system."

Lenny is skeptical. "What makes you so confident? To come up with an enterprise system that brings value we need much more than just the ability to write computer code. We need to know what to program."

"Of course. So what?" Scott asks, forcing Lenny to verbalize his concerns.

"Judging from our experience in production, the key to writing a good system is finding the right rules to follow. We know that it isn't easy to identify the wrong rules. And it's even more difficult to find the new right ones. How are we going to do it?"

"We will, sooner than you think," Scott assures him.

Lenny narrows his eyes. "You know something I don't?"

"No," Scott answers. And then, smiling, he adds, "If you don't include using what we have between our ears."

"Another Sherlock analysis?"

Scott continues to smile. "Not another one, the same analysis. Lenny, you have all the facts. You can figure it out."

Seeing that Lenny is not in the mood, Scott gives in. "The wrong rules will expose themselves," Scott says confidently. Then he explains. "If we've learned anything from our ERP system it's that all functions in an organization are strongly connected to each other. Look at how much information we have to exchange between them.

"We have now incorporated a major change in one function.

What does Maggie call it? A cultural revolution. Since the functions are strongly dependent, and since the other functions didn't change the way they're doing business, it must cause an imbalance. It must be that soon, the changes introduced in one section will clash with the wrong rules that still exist in the other sections. If we're paying attention, we can spot the wrong rules. We just need to keep our eyes open."

Lenny is far from relaxed, but at this stage he doesn't have anything to add.

"I hope you're right," he sighs.

Chapter 15

Maggie turns her eyes from the computer and looks at her assistant. "Patrick, it's getting out of hand," she exclaims. "We're starting to lose control."

"What do you expect when we're launching almost ten projects a day?" Patrick is beat. Not that his work was ever easy. Cleaning up after a tornado like Maggie, making sure that no details are neglected, was never a nine-to-five job. But what's been happening over the last month dwarfs anything he had ever faced before. He is now putting in ninety hours a week and things are nevertheless starting to fall between the cracks.

Nor is Maggie bright-eyed and bushy tailed. The long hours and the number of important decisions that she constantly has to make do take their toll. "Don't exaggerate!" she snaps back. "We don't launch ten projects a day. Look at the numbers."

"I did."

She turns back to the computer, making a few clicks on the mouse. "I already told you, it's not ten," she smiles. "This week we're averaging only eight point five new projects a day."

"I'm so relieved to hear that," Patrick replies sarcastically. Then he says, "From the two competitors who are in trouble, so

161

far we have concentrated on approaching the clients of only POM. You know that we are still learning how to give the offer, nevertheless we have good results. A month ago we were at 10% success, now we have already reached over 20% success."

"But Patrick, let's put things in perspective. Yes, we are launching new projects at an unprecedented rate. However, the vast majority of these projects are small potatoes. Most are simply Drum-Buffer-Rope and Buffer management, in single plants."

"Small potatoes?" Patrick is on the warpath again. "Each one of them requires three to six people. Each one requires a good project manager. Each one requires synchronization with a TOC consultant. To launch and supervise them is not trivial, it's a lot of work."

Maggie doesn't reply. She leans back in her overstuffed, burgundy chair, and gazes at the picture on the wall; the duck picture that Scott gave her. That provokes Patrick more. "Maggie, don't you see what's coming?" His voice increases in pitch. "These projects are only pilots!"

Quickly taking control of himself he continues more calmly. "Judging by the way they're progressing, each one is going to turn, in just two to three months, into a major success. Almost all of them will grow into a much bigger project. What are we going to do then?"

He waits for her to answer but she doesn't. "Besides," he adds, "not all new projects are small. Every other day we launch a full-blown implementation. I don't remember any other time that we were starting so many large projects."

"Yes, Patrick," Maggie finally replies. "We have a lot of healthy problems." Smiling, she asks, "Would you rather be in the opposite situation?"

That stops him. He smiles back, "I didn't say that, but . . ."

Maggie doesn't let him continue. "Let's look at where our difficulties are. Do we have enough people to put on the new projects?"

"We do," he admits. "The arrangement that you reached with the system integrators of POM is brilliant."

"I agree." Maggie cannot resist the temptation to pat herself on the back. And she well deserves it. Before the new year, she had contacted the companies that specialized in implementing POM's software. POM was the first ERP company to report a decline in total sales. It's no wonder that their system implementers were very concerned. Putting herself in their shoes she knew exactly what they were afraid of and what would be an attractive offer for them.

POM, unlike BGSoft, was relying on several smaller system integrator companies which were used in order to promote fierce competition among them. It helped POM to lower prices to its clients without lowering the revenues to POM itself, but it certainly didn't promote loyalty between the system integrators and POM.

Maggie offered them two-year contracts for blocks of a hundred people at a time. The price was high enough to give these companies a hefty margin but it was not even close to the price that KPI is charging its clients. Giving such long-term contracts wasn't a real gamble for Maggie's side, she knew KPI would continue to need many more people for the next two years, and it had several nice side benefits.

She had agreed with Gail to first concentrate on POM's clients as their primary target. Having people who knew exactly the status of POM's implementations and the internal politics turned out to be a big help. Besides, once such a contract was won, the first step always involved conversion from POM's systems. Having people who knew POM's file structure inside and out sped up the implementation. That was very important since these contracts were based on reaching bottom-line results within a short time.

One thing that Maggie is particularly careful about is giving everyone assigned to a "scheduling and execution" project the right orientation. In these projects, the focus is not on making the computer screen look pretty, or making the reports exceptionally "user-friendly." What is important is to make sure that the relevant information will be available for the right people at the right time so that the bottom-line results will be guaranteed. This is quite a paradigm shift for the system integrators.

This reorientation course takes a whole week. The first two days were designed by a TOC consultant, the remaining three days were designed by Lenny.

Maggie presses on. "Do we have a problem with the ability of our people to deliver?"

"Not really," Patrick answers, "we made sure that they have what if takes. Then he adds, "Judging by the progress reports, our people are doing fine on these new projects. Almost every project is on budget and ahead of time. That, in my experience, is unprecedented."

"So what are you complaining about?"

He looks at her, opens his mouth to answer and then regrets it.

"Well?" she insists.

That's too much for Patrick. With a slight touch of sarcasm he replies, "Well, nothing. Everything is just fine Maggie."

"So why are you so furious?"

"I didn't start it," he barely controls himself. "It was you who said that it's getting out of hand, that we're starting to lose control. And I think you're right. Absolutely right. But now if you want to pretend that everything is fine and dandy then that's just fine with me too. You're the boss. Just try not to blame me when the roof caves in on us." In a soft pleading tone, he adds, "Maggie, it's too much. We have to slow down."

"You're right," she admits. "But what can we do? BGSoft can't slow down, and we have to keep up with them."

"Who says that BGSoft can't slow down?" he challenges. "One way or another they'll have to. The question is should they slow down now, or wait until we lose control and drive the implementations into the ground."

She looks at him for a long while. Then she picks up the phone and calls Gail.

"Gail, it's Maggie. How do you stand on that ambitious forecast we submitted for BGSoft?"

"Funny you should ask," comes the answer. "I was about to call you about that exact issue. Maggie, I'm sorry, but I have to ask you to slow down."

"Can I put you on the speaker phone? I'd like Patrick to be a part of this conversation."

"Go ahead." Gail waits for the familiar hum and asks, "Patrick, can you hear me?"

"Yes, Gail, we can hear you fine."

"So, as I just said to Maggie, I'm sorry but I have to ask you guys to stop selling. With what we already have in hand it looks like we're going to exceed our forecast for the quarter. I've already instructed some of my account managers to employ delaying tactics and they're raising hell. I hope that you'll be a little more sensible."

"I'm not sure," says Maggie, while making a face at Patrick.

"Maggie, you of all people should understand me," Gail pleads. "You were the one who helped me convince Scott that jumping to a sixty percent growth rate is not realistic, and that an additional five percent increase every quarter would be good enough."

"And we don't want to lose credibility by proving ourselves wrong," Maggie completes Gail's thought. "Where do we stand now?"

"Counting only things that are signed or are definitely in the bag, and assuming that nothing else comes in, we are going to close the quarter with a forty-seven percent increase. You see what we didn't take into account was that our new strategy would be so powerful in closing new prospects."

"You're right," Maggie says. "We do close large accounts almost every other day. I told you that selling value would be a piece of cake."

"It's not that," Gail objects. "Nothing sells itself, no matter how good it is. It's our new tactics. What really made the difference is your super idea of changing the traditional implementation sequence. No one can compete against an offer that promises a tangible return on investment of less than twelve months."

Maggie enjoys the compliment. "That was just common sense. Why start with the financial modules and drag the client through a tedious and long effort before he sees anything of real value. That makes the client jumpy and causes him to complain about any small hiccup. It's much easier to start with the Drum-Buffer-Rope and Buffer management, demonstrate startling bottom-line results, and then they're so pleased they will forgive us even if we have major overruns on the remaining infrastructure installation."

Gail laughs, "You have your reasons, I have mine. What I care about is that we never had such a high closing ratio and it does seem to shorten the sale cycle. So Maggie will you please go slower on the pilots?"

"I will, Gail. Frankly, we launched so many of them that it's becoming quite chaotic here. And I'm starting to run out of good TOC consultants. But Gail, I don't think that we underestimate the importance of these pilots. We at KPI estimate that at least eighty percent will finish with better results than their benchmarks."

"Who's underestimating them?" Gail protests. "That's actually the main reason I want you to stop. I figured that half the pilots would convert, this year, into full-blown implementations. That will take us way over our target. You've launched almost fifty of those so far. How many more do you have scheduled?"

"If you ignore the pilots that we started in our own clients, and count only those that we launched at our competitor's clients, then you are right. So far we have started forty-eight pilots. As for what we have waiting in the wings, if I count the ones that are practically closed and simply need to agree on the start date, then we're talking about another thirty. I hope that when you say to stop selling you don't mean to stop those? It's too late."

"Can you at least postpone their start dates? And Maggie, one more thing. We're sending too many prospects to Brian at Pierco. I'm afraid that we are overstretching Brian's generosity. Can you just use him for the really strategic sales?"

When Maggie agrees to both requests, Gail continues. "Some more good news. Ordata is offering unreasonable concessions. I won't be surprised if they drop out of the race soon. I already made some inquiries and we may be able to snatch some of their best account managers. Maybe you should start to talk with their system integrators?"

"Thanks for the tip. I will. So other than that, how's life?"

"It's a madhouse here, but I prefer it a hundred times more than what we had last year. That was tough."

"How are Scott and Lenny doing?"

"Lenny is playing with his new toy, multi-project management. I know he's about to buy a company or two. Scott is out most of the time. Rumor has it that he's studying TOC. I really don't know what he's up to, but you know Scott. When he's ready to tell us, he will. But Maggie dear, that's all for the best. Let the men stay out of the way and leave us alone to do the real work. Oops—sorry Patrick."

Chapter 16

"What's wrong with you people? Since when does it take two hours to unload a truck?"

"We don't have all day," another truck driver complains. "How come there's only two of you working?"

"Call for help," roars another.

The forklift operator doesn't bother answering. There's no point arguing with truck drivers. Especially when they have a point. He just lowers the fork a little and moves forward. When the pallet is firmly resting on the big fork he reverses, takes a turn, and drives to the barcode stand. The content is registered and a location is assigned. Within moments the forklift starts the slow journey down one of the long aisles. The truck drivers watch as the big forklift becomes dwarfed in the distance.

It's a big warehouse. Almost six hundred yards long, and most of it already full of Pierco's fine products. The forklift operator doesn't have access to the computer system but he doesn't need the computer to know that for the last two months inventory has been piling up. Now that all the convenient slots are filled he has to drive the long distance all the way to the end. Considering also the time it takes to put the pallet ten

168

yards high, the truck drivers aren't going to see him for some time. It's no wonder they're furious.

When he returns for the next pallet none of the drivers are there. They've probably gone to talk with Fred, the warehouse manager. A lot of good it will do them, he smiles to himself, and carefully aims the fork. No chance that Fred will divert one of the forklifts that loads the vans to help with the unloading. If there's something holy in this warehouse, it's to never allow an outgoing order to wait until the next day. They even stay over-time to guarantee it. Fred's bonus depends on it.

It's ten o'clock at night. The last of the empty trucks drove off a half hour ago. Fred is the only one left in the warehouse. He paces the back of his kingdom looking at the shelves. "Six more yards today," he mutters to himself. That's his way of measuring inventory. Six more yards of his warehouse are full of products.

But that's not his only problem. That's just the most apparent one. The pressure of the truck drivers escalated to such heights that he had to add another forklift to help unload. That had its price. Today was the first time they missed fulfilling all the outgoing orders; almost ten percent of the orders were not shipped to the clients.

Fred can easily remember days when over twenty percent of the orders were not filled, but that was because he didn't have the inventory. Never before had he missed because he didn't have the capacity to load.

Should he use the loading dock at the back for unloading? It wouldn't help much. Almost half of the incoming inventory goes to replace stuff taken from the front of the warehouse. The average distance the forklifts have to travel will not go down by much.

But maybe it's better than nothing. Tomorrow he will look into putting another barcode station at the back of the warehouse.

Still, the time to unload a truck will remain unreasonably

long. The queue of waiting trucks will grow and with it the drivers' impatience and fury. The only way to dramatically lower their waiting time is to unload all the pallets into a nearby area and later move each pallet to its proper place. But that means double handling. Which means a lot more people.

No way, Fred concludes. Two of his prime measurements are already shot to pieces. His inventory turns are at an all-time low and on-time delivery performance is quickly deteriorating. He will not let his cost go way above budget, too. No way.

There's only one way out. The plants must stop shipping so much stuff. All the problems are because they ship him too much. And he can't do a thing about it.

Fred's steps echo as he walks back to his office. He is furious. They have put him in an impossible situation. They're measuring him on things that are not under his control. The plants are going crazy and he's the one who is going to be blamed.

In the past he held about two months of inventory. Maybe a little bit more. Since the beginning of the year his inventory levels have climbed to almost three months. And he still has shortages. There are six products of which he has zero stock. And two dozen more are approaching dangerously low levels. But they keep sending him products he has plenty of. How many items does he have enough of for at least the next six months? He has to check, but there must be over fifty of those.

They don't know what they're doing back there in the plants. And he is helpless. He can't refuse the shipments. He can't tell a truck to take back stuff he doesn't need.

There's only one thing to do. If they want him to be responsible for his inventory turns he must be the one who decides what will be shipped to his warehouse. Not the plants.

It's about time to do something about it. At the rate things are going, in a month the warehouse will be jam-packed. What are they going to do then? Tell him to store the inventory in the parking lot?

Fred decides to do something he has never done before, he is going to send a strong e-mail directly to the divisional VP. On second thought, he decides to also CC all the plant managers. These people had better wake up.

Harrison is in his office staring through the glass wall down to his plant floor. As far as the eye can see there are rows of machines with a few people scattered here and there. The thick glass blocks mask most of the noise and to Harrison the view looks peaceful. Compared to what it was before, it is peaceful down there. No more frantic expediting, no more jumping from one emergency to another. Not since they implemented the Drum-Buffer-Rope system. Such a logical step. Why hadn't they done it a long time ago?

But, life is always complicated. If things are going well here, then someone has to stir up problems somewhere else. That Fred, or whatever his name is, had stirred up a whole hornets' nest. In the last two days since his ridiculous e-mail arrived, a few more warehouse managers had raised their heads. What do they think? That they can run his plant for him? Tell him what to produce? Tell him what to ship?

And all their complaints are based on nothing. When you strip away all the nitpicking that they wrote, it's clear that all their complaints are based on one single claim. The claim that the plants produce and ship things that the warehouses don't need. And that claim is outrageous.

He just spent hours verifying that the opposite is true. In the last three months, production has been triggered by an urgent demand from at least one of the warehouses. There was not a single case where his plant produced a product that was not frantically demanded by a warehouse. Not even one.

Of course when they produce a product, they don't produce it for just one warehouse. They produce the quantity needed for the entire network. Otherwise the plant will have to produce ridiculously small quantities and the setup will swallow too much capacity. True, since they had moved to Drum-Buffer-Rope they no longer had to try to save cost by running large batches. The batches processed are now less than half of what they used to run, many times, fewer than a quarter. But still, when the plant produces these smaller quantities, setup is an issue.

Harrison knows that his people are not dumb; that they are shipping the products to the warehouses that need them. Nevertheless, he spent quite a lot of time on the computer checking the last three months' history. As he fully expected, the products were being shipped to the right places. Obviously, when the amount sent to a warehouse was not enough to fill a truck the quantities were rounded up. If his people had not done that, he could imagine the reaction. Sending half-empty trucks is not acceptable at Pierco, or anywhere else.

An hour later Harrison examines the memo he wrote to Brian, the divisional vice president. He is not happy with it. The memo is not strong enough, and it's too defensive. Something is missing.

He rereads it. And then he rereads the memos of the warehouse managers. He tries to see what is likely to be the reaction of a person who doesn't know all the intricacies. A person like Brian.

As much as he hates to admit it, his memo is not enough to fully answer the warehouses' complaints. No wonder, his mistake is that he aims his attack against something that they never wrote explicitly. In all their memos they were careful not to directly blame the plants for producing the wrong products. They just alluded to it.

What is it that gives that impression? What puts the blame on the plants?

Once he asks himself these questions it's not difficult to find the answer. Their strongest argument is that for many products, the quantities held in the warehouse are much larger than the targeted level. As a rule they replenish inventory to a level of four months But Fred, for example, attached a list of fifty-four products of which, in his warehouse, there is more than six months of inventory.

How can it be? Now that the ERP is providing them with up-to-date data about the actual inventories in the warehouses, they don't have to guess anymore. They are shipping the exact amounts. If all the plants are as careful as he is not to send above the four months' mark, how come there are so many products with so much inventory?

He turns to the computer to checks Fred's claims. Twelve of the products that appear in Fred's list are his products. And yes, their inventory levels are much too high. How come?

Harrison starts to dig. He concentrates on the product with the highest inventory level. What was its inventory in Fred's warehouse when this product was last shipped to him? He has never before asked the system such a question, so it takes some time, and a few frustrating dead ends, before he figures out a way to get the answer.

The last time that this product was shipped to Fred was on the seventh of January, about nine weeks ago. At that time the inventory at Fred's warehouse was sufficient for just two weeks of future sales. The quantity shipped from Harrison's plant raised it to exactly four months. Since then no additional product was sent. Still the system now claims that the inventory level is at eight months. Something must be terribly wrong with the system.

Before he calls the IT department and starts to raise hell, Harrison decides to check another possibility. Maybe Fred, in his fear of running out of inventory, asked for a cross shipment from another warehouse? That could explain what happened. These warehouse managers mess things up with their own hands and then blame the plants. How typical. But how can he prove it? The only way is to enter the distribution system.

Harrison isn't familiar with that part of the computer system, so everything takes much more time. Finally he figures out how to ask for all the movement of that product at Fred's warehouse. The list is endless. Most of it is totally irrelevant to what he is looking for. It's the shipment of small quantities from the warehouse to the clients.

He rolls down the list until he reaches the seventh of January.

He identifies the line of the shipment from his plant, but what he is looking for are shipments to Fred's warehouse from other warehouses. He cannot find any, not even when he goes back as far as the beginning of December. But on the list there is also a different type of line, one that sheds a new light on the entire picture.

These are the lines that update, once a month, the forecast for the product. Harrison leans back in his chair. He should have predicted it. If there is a mess in operations, rest assured that it was caused by corporate.

On the first of February the forecast for the sales of this product in Fred's region was lowered to about one half. On the first of March it was lowered again. No wonder that the inventory, since it is measured by future months of sales, is now at the level of eight months. Production was right. Shipping was right. The problem is the forecast.

Harrison goes over the other eleven products just to verify that the exact same phenomena exist. Now he's ready to rewrite his memo to Brian. Now it is going to have the effect he wants. It will, no doubt, remove the possibility that the warehouses will get more control over the plants. His memo is going to be so powerful because it also provides a solution. It clearly indicates whom to blame.

Brian stares at the e-mail sent to him by the chief financial officer of Pierco. It is short and demanding.

You are draining the cash of Pierco. In January your division was over budget by forty-five million dollars. In February by an additional fifty-two million dollars. You must reverse this devastating trend.

This memo is not entirely a surprise to Brian, he is well aware of the rate cash is drained by the increase in inventory. The only thing that is slightly surprising is how quickly they came to him. Well, even that's not really a surprise. This new ERP system gives better visibility not just to him but also to corporate.

It's been quite some time since he noticed that inventories

are climbing. At first he brushed it aside as an end-of-the-year effect. Now he knows that it's rapidly developing into a major catastrophe. He also knows where it's coming from. It's coming from the fact that the Drum-Buffer-Rope implementations have released so much hidden capacity in the plants. When the plants are producing over forty percent more than before and sales stay about the same, then the unavoidable result is a sharp and continuous increase in inventory. That is clear. What is not clear to Brian is what to do about it.

He doesn't need the memo from headquarters to tell him that he must do something. Do something drastic and do it fast.

At first he thought that he had a simple and elegant solution. Whenever the plants are shipping products to the warehouses the current measurement system rewards the plants with an internal sale. Whether or not the products are actually needed at the warehouses is not a factor the measurement system considers. The plants are rewarded in any case. So Brian thought that he could stop the accumulation of the unneeded inventories by simply modifying the measurement system.

Acknowledging an internal sale only if the shipment was done to a warehouse that needed the products would stop the plants from producing just to score high on their measurement, stop them from producing what is not needed by distribution.

The power of the ERP system, its processing speed, and the fact that all the relevant information is available, made such a modification possible. It was implemented in less than two weeks.

But it didn't have any effect, the inventories continued to rise.

As it turned out the plants were producing only products for which there was demand from distribution. Actually, each product that the plants produced was in response to an urgent demand from a warehouse; a real shortage or something that was about to become short.

That was a big surprise to Brian. Not that the plants are doing what should be done, he knew that his plant managers looked at the good of the system as a whole, but he was not prepared for the fact that there were so many shortages.

Shortages did go down. Less than a year ago, before the ERP was implemented in distribution, shortages were encountered in about fifteen percent of incoming orders. With the implementation of ERP, shortages dropped to a little over ten percent. The increase in capacity in the plants did have an additional impact. It reduced shortages to less than four percent and considerably reduced the need for cross shipments between warehouses. What was a mystery to Brian was why there was so much more inventory and nevertheless still significant shortages. Enough to force the plants to constantly react.

He struggled with that puzzle. It took him quite a while to figure out the answer.

Even though the trigger to produce is a shortage in one warehouse, a plant cannot afford to produce just for one warehouse. So the plant produces and ships to other warehouses too. These shipments are done to increase inventory in warehouses from, let's say, a level of six weeks to the targeted level of four months. Which means that most of the inventories are shipped based on a forecast of what is expected to be sold many weeks from now. And that forecast is far from being reliable.

Actually, who's talking about reliability here, the sale's forecast for a product in a single region is outright lousy. No wonder that they end up with too much inventory in many places and not enough in others. Which translates, when one deals with over six hundred products and over two dozen regional warehouses into having shortages.

They must have a better forecast. That's the only way to eliminate the shortages. That's the only way to stop the buildup of excess inventories.

Their new ERP system has a fancy forecasting module, with many more features then they ever had before. Still, the validity of the resulting forecast is not improved. In this aspect their new ERP system has let them down.

Last week he spoke with George. At first George tried to claim that BGSoft's forecasting module is the best there is. Then he tried to duck responsibility, but Brian knew how to light a fire under him. No matter how difficult it is, BGSoft must come up with a much better forecasting module. It's essential.

Brian wonders about the chances that BGSoft experts will come up with an accurate forecast. Is it possible at all to have an accurate forecast? Besides, even if they would pull it off, there is no time left. He must do something now.

He looks again at the memo:

In January your division was over budget by forty-five million dollars. In February by an additional fifty-two million dollars.

As things are progressing he is destined to drain at least another sixty million dollars in March. Then what will be headquarters' reaction? He shivers just thinking about it.

He must do something to stop the cash drain now. Even if what he does is stupid for the long run. He must stop the plants from producing.

Actually, the whole situation is grotesque. The plants have exposed much more capacity. They are able to react much better to the distribution needs. But as a result the situation is rapidly deteriorating. That doesn't make any sense.

There must be something fundamentally wrong with what they're doing. Things are worse than before. But having more capacity without the need to pay for it is good. Nobody can tell him otherwise.

With that conviction in mind, Brian's thoughts drift back to basics. All the shipments of products to the warehouses are based on replenishing to targeted levels. The targeted inventory levels in distribution are fixed to four months. It's been this way for as long as he can remember. Also, for as long as he can remember, the average inventory in their distribution oscillated around half of the target; around the two-months mark. But that is changing now. Actual inventory levels are rapidly growing. At the end of this quarter the average inventory level will be three months or more.

He tries to summarize it. The plants' capabilities improved. As a result the inventories and the warehouses are moving closer to their targeted levels. And that's why he has problems? How can it be?

Then it dawns on him. It is so embarrassingly simple. The target is wrong! The targeted inventory levels are wrong!

Brian smiles bitterly to himself. The targeted inventory levels were established years ago, based on the capabilities of the system. Based on the average time it took to replenish the inventory that was sold from the warehouses. In the last year they significantly improved the speed at which the system can replenish the warehouses. And yet, no one thought about the obvious, the fact that faster replenishment to distribution means that there is no need to target such high inventories in the warehouses.

This "small" oversight has turned an opportunity to lower inventories into a reality in which inventories are rapidly climbing.

Well, now he knows what to do. The plants can now react in about half the time, so the target for the inventory levels should be cut in half.

He doesn't have to do anything more. He doesn't have to instruct the plants to stop producing. The change that he has done in the plant's measurement will guarantee it. The new measurement is no longer a reward for shipments of products that are not needed in a warehouse, therefore reducing the targeted levels will stop the plants from over-producing. That will stop the buildup of inventories in the warehouses. As a matter of fact, cutting the targets to only two months will force inventories to go down to a lower level than ever before. It will reverse the trend. Cash will be released. Corporate will be off his back. He will be a hero.

Pleased with himself, Brian starts to write e-mails to all the relevant people, instructing the targeted levels to be cut in half. This is not a trivial task. He knows that he is changing something that is part of the fabric. He must explain every aspect meticulously. Otherwise he will trigger a lot of confusion, mis-interpretations, and even anger.

What will be the reaction of the plant managers? They will claim that reducing the targeted levels will force them into much too small production runs. In a way that's correct, but it can't be a real problem. Brian decides to devote some time to figuring out how he can put this claim to rest.

In the past, when in one warehouse there was a shortage, in the other warehouses the gap between the actual inventory and the targeted inventory was, on average, two months. That meant that the plant had a production run of about two months consumption of the whole market.

But now, when the target inventories are lowered to just two months, when there is a shortage in one warehouse, most other warehouses don't need any additional product. And those few warehouses where the inventory is less than two months, the amount missing is probably just a week or two. Too small a quantity to fill even half a truck.

That means, Brian starts to realize in panic, that the average production run will be just for two months for one warehouse. That is about four percent of the traditional production runs. Knowing that set-up is about ten percent of the total time, it is clear to Brian that such small production runs will cause set-ups to absorb almost all the capacity. The plant will be left with less than half the capacity they had before. They will not be able to produce at the rate of sales.

So cutting the targeted inventories is not a good answer, not when he considers the impact it will have on products' availability in the next quarter. Deeply disappointed, Brian realizes that he is back to square one. The answer must be to drastically improve the forecast. But right now he doesn't have a choice. He must act.

When he finishes writing the e-mails that cut the targeted levels he picks up the phone and calls George.

George puts down the phone and grabs his head with both hands. What is he going to do now?

Brian is putting the squeeze on him to install a forecasting module that accurately forecasts future sales. After a whole week of frantic memos and phone calls he at last succeeded in getting a hold of Lenny. Just to hear that Lenny is not going to collaborate. Lenny practically laughed in his face. He said that there was no way to forecast accurately, weeks in advance, the market demand of a single product in a single region. It is theoretically impossible.

George doesn't understand Lenny's exact explanations but he does understand that BGSoft is not going to make any attempt to provide a better forecasting module.

What made him choose to work in this lousy job? Whatever he does is not good enough. Over and over again he finds himself under the gun for something he doesn't have any control over.

He worked his butt off on Pierco's implementation. He had to constantly struggle with unreasonable requests from clients, with slow response of the software programmers, with bugs, with mismatches in the ERP system. After years of relentless efforts it looked like he had succeeded in making it all work. He managed to turn this huge, complicated project into the jewel in the crown of KPI, into the best reference site.

But that's all over.

Brian made it clear that unless the forecast accuracy is significantly improved, he will not entertain any more visits from KPI prospects, that he cannot recommend a system that is directly responsible for an increase of over a hundred million dollars in inventory. He also hinted that he is going to raise the issue with all the other divisional vice presidents of Pierco. And Lenny, the only person who can do something about it, doesn't even want to listen.

George has had it. He decides to pass the buck and drop this in Maggie's lap. Maybe she can knock some sense into Lenny. He doesn't care. He wants to be transferred to another project.

The flight attendant takes away Maggie's food tray. Maggie can now go back to her e-mails. The next one up is from George.

George always has good news. Not to mention the fact that he uses witty language when he reports on the visits of the prospects to Pierco. She smiles as she double clicks to open his e-mail.

Her smile doesn't last for long.

Gail was right all along. They should have stuck to selling technology. Here is the software, these are the specs. The software operates according to the specs. Good. I've done my job, everybody is happy. But no, they had to go into selling value. What a mistake!

Brian asked for software for production. BGSoft supplied the software. KPI installed it. Successfully. The software works, results have been achieved. Astonishing results. Can they relax now? Can they feel that they've done a good job and everybody is happy? Not at all.

Here they are, three months later, and it's blown up in their faces. And not because something went bad in production. In production everything is fine and dandy.

Results are deteriorating in distribution by 100 million dollars and they are being blamed. That's the meaning of selling value. There are no boundaries to what you are responsible for.

A hundred million dollars. If that story goes out, Maggie can easily envision what it will do. Now that the competition is so envious of BGSoft and KPI, they will not hesitate to use it, to broadcast it from every rooftop. It's one thing to have a bad reference. It's another thing when your best reference, the one you used the most, the one that you brought dozens of prospects to see, turns into your worst nightmare.

Can she persuade Brian to keep the lid on it? Only if she can promise that they are working hard on a solution. But that means forcing Lenny to give it a shot.

That definitely won't be easy. Not when Lenny is convinced that he cannot provide better software. Damn it, why can't he go through the motions? No one expects a new software module to be developed in less than six months. In six months, Brian is bound to find a solution. Some non-software solution.

Determined to put full pressure on Lenny, she returns to George's e-mail. What exactly does she have to ask of Lenny?

Reading George's message a second time, Maggie growls as she realizes the magnitude of the problem. It is by far bigger then she originally thought.

Keeping the lid on Pierco will not help at all. What's happening in Brian's division is not a fluke, it is not one unfortunate case. It is a warning of what is waiting for them from all sides.

George is quite explicit about the fact that Brian is not pointing the finger at them for no reason. It's their software that helped expose so much hidden capacity in the plants. And when production goes way up and sales lags behind, the unavoidable result is a continuous increase in the inventory in distribution. It's not a problem in plants that produce to orders, but it's an unavoidable problem in plants that produce to forecast. Finished goods inventories will go up.

In how many other plants that feed distribution have they installed the new production software? It's about half of the projects that they have launched this year.

And in these dozens of projects, since their implementations in production are almost always successful in increasing capacity, the same thing will happen. Inventories will grow and they will be blamed for it.

She can hide one case. Maybe even two or three. But not dozens. What a name they'll get! No company will touch their software with a ten-foot pole. They are doomed.

A minute later, she reaches for her briefcase determined to catch the next flight back. Scott must hear about it, and this is not a subject to be discussed over the phone.

Chapter 17

MARCH 18, 1999

"I hope you know what you're doing," Maggie can't restrain herself from whispering to Scott as he stands up and walks to the podium.

Scott shakes Craig's hand, thanks him for the introduction, and turns to face the audience.

Pierco's small auditorium is almost full. Brian's memo to all the other divisional VPs, followed by the memo from the chief financial officer, must have raised a real concern. Otherwise it is difficult to find an explanation for how this gathering had been arranged at such short notice. Present in the auditorium are not just all the divisional vice presidents, but all the plant managers of Pierco and almost all the warehouse managers also.

Scott knows that he is addressing a potentially hostile audience. These people are concerned about what they are hearing from Brian's division. Word spreads quickly, and it is natural for them to blame what they consider to be a BGSoft initiative. It is essential for Scott to divert the hostility, to turn the situation from "you against us," into "you and us against the problem."

Calmly, in a factual tone, he begins. "Last quarter the divi-

sion headed by Brian started to implement the production application of the Theory of Constraints in all their seven plants.
May I ask the plant managers of these plants to identify themselves?"

A cluster of people on the very left side of the third and forth
rows raise their hands.

Scott looks at them and asks, "Did you get results?"

Two or three answer, "Yes."

That's not good enough for Scott. He must establish that this
situation is very different from what people are used to. It is not
a case where the company faces problems due to an incorrect
action or lack of actions; it is not a case where they have to find
someone to blame.

"I can't hear you," Scott replies. "Let me try again." And
putting his hand close to his ear he repeats loudly, "Did you get
results?"

The seven plant managers know that Scott is trying to defend BGSoft. But they are also aware that it helps them. It re-
moves the possibility that they will be blamed for what they
have done. Being genuinely proud of their achievement, they
roar in unison, "YES!"

Scott now knows he is standing on solid ground, so he
doesn't hesitate to press on. "Is it true, that without adding any
machines or manpower, you are now able to produce at least
forty percent more than before?"

They look at each other. "Yes," comes the confident answer.

That answer has its impact. The auditorium buzzes. Scott
doesn't hurry to continue. He waits until he has everybody's
attention. Then he asks, "Would you consider going back to the
old methods? To the way the plants were run before?"

They don't hesitate to enthusiastically answer that there is
no way, or reason, to go back.

Satisfied, Scott continues, making eye contact with people all
over the auditorium. "Since the beginning of the year," he
states, "most plants in Pierco started to implement Drum-

Buffer-Rope and Buffer management. I'm sure that those that started in January are already beginning to see some results."

Confirmation comes from several places.

Scott knows that at least the plant managers are now on his side. It's time to expose the problem. But he must be careful to do it in a way that assures everyone that the finger is not going to be pointed at them.

In a stern voice Scott declares, "That major improvement in production has a nasty side effect." He pauses and then continues, "In the first two months of this year sales has to be congratulated for increasing market share by two points. But when you consider the fact that the plants are increasing their production by forty percent, what is the unavoidable result?"

He waits a while before he verbalizes the answer. "The unavoidable result is that inventories are creeping up."

Now he turns to the chief financial officer, sitting in the first row, and asks, "By how much are inventories up?"

The CFO stands up, and turning to face the group, he says, "Since the beginning of the year, inventories are up by over a hundred and fifty million dollars. My calculations show that unless something is done to stop the overproduction, inventories will continue to climb at the alarming rate of more than two hundred million dollars a month. Let me tell you, that no matter how financially strong we are, we cannot afford such a drain of cash." He continues to look at the audience for a while and then states, "We have a problem!" He slowly sits down.

Raising his voice, Scott repeats, "We definitely have a problem." And then he adds, "The increase in inventories is due to the increase in capacity of the plants. But where do the inventories accumulate? In distribution. Just ask the warehouse managers how frustrating it is to be in charge of increasing inventories without the power to do anything about it. Distribution owns the problem but they didn't cause it and they can't do a thing about it."

Judging by the response Scott knows that he has now also won over the warehouse managers. It is time to move on and debate the possible solutions. People tend to resist radical solutions, and the solution he has to offer is very radical. Yesterday they put their heads together to find the most suitable way of presenting it, Craig, Brian, Maggie and himself. They debated it for hours. It wasn't difficult to agree that the best way would be to unfold the solution by deriving it through questions and answers. The debate was on the mechanism to use. Brian suggested a way. Craig and Scott liked it but Maggie forcefully objected. But they wore her down. Then Brian and Scott spent the better part of the night rehearsing. Now they were going to see if it worked.

First Scott has to set the ground. "So what are we going to do about it?" Scott asks his audience. He continues immediately, "Your chief financial officer has suggested a simple solution. You heard the man. What he is saying is 'stop the overproduction.' Don't dismiss it. Why won't you stop the production of products that just accumulate in the warehouses?"

Several plant managers are trying to answer at the same time. The warehouse managers apparently don't agree with them. Within less than a minute it is impossible to hear anybody anymore.

It takes Scott a few minutes to quiet them down enough to say, "I think we should have representation of both camps on the stage."

As they expected, when the CEO and all the VPs are present, nobody volunteers.

Smiling, Scott says, "Since no one volunteers, let me use the army method. Brian, you are volunteered. Come up here." Turning to the audience Scott adds, "Being a vice president in charge of both production and distribution, Brian can fairly represent both groups. Beside, he's the one who started all this mess."

"This is rehearsed," Scott reveals to the audience while Brian clips a microphone to his shirt.

When he is ready, Scott starts to "interview" him.

What they agreed on is that they should not make the mistake of assuming that most managers in the room understand the situation to the degree that Brian does. They haven't spent as much time trying to figure out a solution. So first Scott and Brian have to deepen the audience's understanding.

"Brian, are you familiar with the problem of the sharp increase in inventories?"

Brian, not used to playing a role, cannot hide a smile. "Are you kidding? Out of the hundred and fifty million dollars that were mentioned here, almost a hundred belongs to my division."

"So I guess that you've thought about this problem?"

"In the last month I haven't thought about anything but this problem."

"Yes, I can see the steam coming out of your ears," Scott remarks and then raises the question everybody is waiting for. "So why don't you stop the overproduction?"

"What do you call overproduction?" Brian asks.

"I assume that for each product in each warehouse there are target inventory levels."

Brian agrees. "Traditionally the targeted levels in my division are fixed to four months consumption."

"So overproduction," Scott answers, "is producing and shipping above these targeted levels."

"If this is your definition of overproduction," Brian says, looking directly at the CFO, "then none of my plants have ever overproduced."

Scott pretends that he is surprised. "So how come inventories are going up?"

Brian explains. "In the past, the actual inventories were at the level of about two months. Now they are closer to three months. Still below the targeted levels."

"I see." Scott sounds puzzled. "So, you say there was no overproduction?"

"Depends what you call overproduction," Brian answers. "I define it as producing and shipping inventories that don't help the warehouses to better service the clients."

"Sounds reasonable," Scott agrees. "But isn't it the same as what I said? Weren't the targeted levels set to be in line with the amount needed to service the clients?"

"Yes, in the past," Brian answers. "But since the plants are now getting the information about the stocks in each warehouse in almost real time, and since the plants have dramatically increased their capacity, the situation has changed. The time from a request by a warehouse until it's filled has dropped, on average, to almost half. As a result, the targeted levels should be cut in half."

"Fine," says Scott. "Cut the targeted inventory levels in half and don't overproduce relative to these new levels."

"We did, a week ago," Brian answers.

"And inventory still continues to accumulate?"

"No. The trend has been reversed, inventories in my division are starting to take a nose dive."

"So what's the problem?" Scott performs like a real actor. "Why was I called here?"

"Because not overproducing, relative to the new targeted levels, does have its price." In a dramatic tone Brian adds, "A price so high that I think the medicine may be worse than the illness."

"What price? What are you talking about?"

"Shortages," Brian answers laconically.

"Shortages?" Scott plays his part. "But I thought you said that you have too much inventory. Where did shortages come from?"

"For each product in the distribution system there is plenty of inventory. A shortage means that a specific product is missing in a specific warehouse. At the end of February we had only one hundred-thirty-two shortages. In the last week, the net number of shortages has been increasing by about twenty a day. You ask where the shortages are coming from? Well Scott, you also asked why we called you here. So let me tell you, the shortages are a direct result of your ERP system."

Scott takes a step back and raises his hands as if to defend himself. "Hold your horses. In what way does my ERP system create your shortages?"

Seeing Scott's act, Brian struggles to hold back another smile. But without missing a beat he continues. "Isn't it obvious? We reduced the targeted inventory levels, from four months to two months. But we still ship inventories from the plants to the warehouses based on forecasted consumption, which is many weeks in the future. And Scott, I'm sorry to be the one to tell you, but the forecast that your ERP provides is lousy."

The room is filled with murmurs of agreement. Yesterday, they had speculated that by now everybody would be blaming the forecast. Everybody see's the solution in getting a better forecast. So before they can start to talk about their solution they have to first remove that dead end. They had planned to make a big fuss about the current state of the forecast.

Brian does not forget his line. Aggressively he says, "The forecast that we get from your ERP system is almost as lousy as the forecast of the temperature weeks in advance." That triggers a lot of laughter.

Scott waits for it to quiet down and with a broad smile says, "No, Brian, it's not nearly as lousy as the weather forecast. It is exactly as lousy as the weather forecast."

When he can be heard again he continues. "The lousy forecast is not a deficiency of the BGSoft computer system. The truth is that it is theoretically impossible to accurately predict the consumption of a specific product in a specific region weeks in advance. Exactly like it is theoretically impossible to forecast temperatures weeks in advance. The software is good enough just to predict trends, nothing more."

Scott waits for this important information to sink in before he continues. "But Brian, you have lots of experience with the Theory of Constraints in production. If you're worried about the forecast, why don't you adopt the TOC application for distribution?"

"I wasn't aware there was an application for distribution. Tell us more."

"Well, it utilizes the fact that the relative forecast accuracy is different for different places in the company. One should hold most of the inventory in the places that have the most accurate forecast."

"I don't understand you," Brian responds. Then he turns to face the audience and asks, "Do you understand what he's saying?"

Almost everybody assures him that they don't.

"What is so difficult to understand?" Scott innocently asks. "Don't you know that the forecast accuracy deteriorates when you're asking for a forecast on a smaller and smaller sample? For a single shop the sales next week might easily be three times bigger or smaller than the sales this week, it is impossible to forecast. But such drastic changes are highly unlikely for the total sales in all shops in North America.

"Correct," Brian agrees. "So what?"

"So I think that it makes sense to hold the inventories at the places where the relevant forecast for them is the forecast for the entire continent; it is by far more accurate."

Brian asks, "And where are those places?"

"The plants," Scott answers. "A plant produces for the whole continent. Why not hold most of the inventory right there, where it's produced?"

"Scott," Brian replies, "maybe what you suggest makes sense, but I'm sure that most people in this room will say that you don't understand our business. In our business finished goods inventory are not held at the plants. You see, we built the distribution system because we have to hold the inventories close to our clients. They will not wait for us to ship it from the plant. When they ask for our products they expect to have it delivered the same day."

"I know," Scott assures him and the rest of the audience. "I know that in your business you aren't holding finished goods inventory at the plants. But it could be the thing to do?"

"You'll have to work very hard to convince us," Brian says decisively.

Scott asks, "Can I at least try?"

"Be my guest."

"Brian, you said that the number of shortages is now increasing at the alarming rate of an additional twenty a day."

"That's right."

"Why?" Scott asks, and quickly adds, "And don't tell me that all of a sudden the accuracy of the forecast dramatically deteriorated."

"No, not at all. The forecast accuracy remained as lousy as before. The rapid increase in shortages is a direct result of the fact that we drastically lowered the targeted inventories. What's happening is that when there's a shortage in one warehouse there's no point in producing the same product for other warehouses as well. Simply put we won't be able to ship it to them. The amount that they need, those that need it at all, is far short of a truckload. The result is that our plants are now producing in tiny production runs. So small that the majority of the time they are busy setting up the lines. It's no wonder that we're falling more and more behind in responding to the warehouses' requests."

"I understand," Scott says. After a second, he says, "but I don't understand."

"What don't you understand?"

"I don't understand why, once a plant needs to produce a product for one warehouse, it doesn't produce five time as much? Ship whatever is needed to the warehouse that asked for it and keep the rest in the plant. How long will it take until other warehouses demand that product and all of it will be shipped? Two weeks? Three?"

Brian pretends to think about it. "We never held finished goods at the plants but, offhand, I don't see why it wouldn't work." He turns to his plant managers. "What do you think?"

One of them replies, "I don't know if I have enough storage space."

"Suppose we solve that problem," Brian says. "We'll find you space nearby. Actually, we could arrange to use the warehouse, which is only about an hour away. Then what do you think about this idea?"

"Makes perfect sense to me," he answers.

"Brian," says another of his plant managers, "We're going crazy producing these small quantities. Anything is better than the present situation. But are you serious? Are you going to allow us to hold finished goods at the plants?"

"Give me one reason why not?"

"I don't know. Company rules maybe?"

Brian just waves his hand in dismissal, and turning to Scott, he says. "I'll have to discuss it more with my people, but for now let's say that it is a good idea."

The groundwork is done. Time to get to the heart of their solution.

Scott controls his desire to cross his fingers behind his back, and begins. "So if holding inventories at the plant might be a good idea, why don't we take it a step further. As we said, the best forecast is at the plant level. What will happen if we held at the plant, let's say, three weeks of inventory of every product it manufactures. What will happen then?"

Before people can start to formulate objections in their heads, Scott continues. "Think about it. The plants won't ever need to produce small quantities. And much more important, look at the service the plants will be able to give the warehouses. If all products are available at the plant then the plant is able to replenish each warehouse on a daily basis. It will be economically feasible. The quantities of each product a warehouse sells per day are small, but if you consider all products a warehouse gets from one plant, these daily quantities are enough to fill up a truck."

"Let me digest," Brian, playing his role, summarizes and explains the solution. "Each plant will be producing its products to fill its own plant warehouse. The regional warehouses will no longer issue orders to fill up inventories to their targeted levels. Rather, whatever a warehouse sells will be shipped to it from the plant warehouse, the next morning. Scott, what you're suggesting is almost the opposite of what we currently do. Today we push the products from the plants to the warehouses as soon as we produce them. According to what you say we should switch from push to pull. Inventories are held at the plants and are pulled from them only according to what was actually sold to the clients."

"Precisely," Scott confirms. "So what do you think?"

"I think I can see the potential, but my mind is full of annoying questions. I'm sure that it's the same for everybody here. So, Scott, let's ask them?"

As Craig predicted, the chief financial officer is the first to raise his hand. "I'm sorry, but I thought that the whole purpose of today was to find an acceptable way to lower the inventories. What I think I'm hearing now is the opposite. Do you really suggest building more warehouses to be filled with inventory?"

Scott and Brian are well prepared for this question.

"I see where you get the impression that I'm suggesting an increase in the inventories Pierco has to hold," Scott answers. "But that's not the case. I'm actually suggesting a way to significantly reduce the total inventory."

"That's what I want to hear," says the CFO.

"Sounds like a miracle," Scott smiles at him. "We add, but the total amount is going down. Strange. To understand how such a miracle happens we have to understand the impact the plant warehouse will have on the level of inventories each regional warehouse will have to hold." Turning to Brian he says, "Help me here. How do you determine the target inventory levels in the regional warehouses?"

"It's actually quite simple," Brian answers. "It's dictated by the replenishment time. If the time to replenish a product to the warehouse is, let's say, six weeks, then theoretically we should target six weeks of inventory. Of course, since the market fluctuates, we should hold more than that, something like ten weeks."

"So why did you target four months?"

"Because we don't start to replenish when an item is sold. The warehouses order only when the inventory reaches some minimum level. Besides, you also have to bear in mind the fact that the time to replenish is not actually known. The plant may get orders for many products all at once and the replenishment time may double."

"I see," says Scott. "So if all products will be available at the plant, what would you say the targeted levels in the regional warehouses should be?"

"Under such conditions the replenishment time will be reduced to just the shipping time," Brian starts to answer. "Not only is it much shorter than what we're used to, it is also much more reliable. For some warehouses it means replenishment time of two or three days. For them, targeted levels of one week would be safe. For the majority of the cases the shipping time is less than one week. I think that it would be safe to say that on average, we are talking about targeted inventories of less than two weeks. And this will be enough to offer service levels that the industry is not accustomed to."

"Fine." Scott is pleased. "Brian, let me stress a point here. You are used to a big gap between the targeted levels of inventory and the actual levels. You target four months and you actually hold about two months. In the new way such a gap does not exist. Targeting two weeks at a regional warehouse and replenishing from the plants on a daily basis means that between the inventory in the warehouse and the inventory on the trucks, you'll actually hold two weeks of inventory."

"Yes," Brian confirms.

"What about the target levels in the plants' warehouses?"

"Three weeks are more than enough," Brian says confidently. And then summarizes, "That means that between the inventories in the plant warehouses, on the roads, and in the regional warehouses, we're talking about five weeks max."

He looks at the CFO. "Even relative to what we held before the inventories started to rise, it means release of more than five hundred million dollars in cash, while practically putting an end to cross shipments and shortages."

"I would like it," is the CFO's response.

Many hands are raised. Brain is looking for a warehouse manager. He signals to one.

"My warehouse is in Kentucky. I'm only a few days drive from all the plants of my division."

"Good for you," Scott interrupts him. "That means that you'll have to hold very low inventories. Your inventory turns will skyrocket."

The warehouse manager doesn't look overly impressed. "I'm concerned about my people. If I have to hold much lower inventories, what will happen to my people?"

"You'll still sell the same amount to your region," Scott reminds him. "The change that we are discussing here will not effect the amount of traffic through your warehouse."

Brian steps forward. "The drastic reduction of inventory will mean that you use only a fraction of the space of your warehouse. That will, no doubt, increase the efficiency of handling things. But on the other hand, you'll have to deal with many more types of products coming to you every day from the plants. I predict that many pallets will be composed of more than one product. That will increase the load on your people. All in all, it's probably a wash. Your people's jobs are safe."

The warehouse manager looks satisfied. Scott turns to choose the next person, when Brian deviates from their "script" and says to the warehouse manager, "I have a question for you. Right now you are the one issuing orders for products to be shipped to your warehouse. Do you understand that what is suggested here will change that?"

"Yes," comes the answer. "I will not issue any orders but whatever I ship to the clients will automatically be shipped to me the next day."

"And that's okay with you?" Brian is surprised. "Giving up so much power?"

"What power? We issue orders now, but who's paying attention to them? Let's face it, the plants produce and ship to us whatever they want. We can't even ship back things that we didn't ask for. No, if they'll ship to me every day what I sold the previous day, that's good enough. Frankly, it sounds like paradise."

"Fine," says Brian. To Scott he says, "You know that our computer system doesn't work this way. It's based on issuing orders from the warehouses, on min-max trigger levels, et cetera. A lot of changes will be needed."

"It's okay," Scott assures him. "The code is ready the minute Pierco decides, we can install it within less than two weeks. That's not the problem."

"Yes," Brian agrees, "I'm sure that people here have much bigger problems to discuss."

"I have a problem," says a large, serious man. "I want to know who's going to determine the levels of inventories the plant has to hold?"

"I gather that you are a plant manager and you don't want anybody messing with your plant? Especially not corporate," Scott sarcastically states.

"Right on," comes the answer from several sides.

"Well," says Scott, "let's look at what we do want. We want that whatever a regional warehouse sells will be sitting ready in the plant warehouse for immediate replenishment. That the plant warehouse will never run out of inventory of any product. That means that the plant has to hold enough inventories to provide enough time to react to whatever the sales will be. What determines the reaction time of the plant? The capabilities it has; its available capacity, its agility, the magnitude of mishaps, et cetera. Who knows it best? The plant."

"So the plant itself will decide how much inventory to hold?"

"That's the idea," Brian assures the plant manager. "But, of course, the plant will be measured on its performance."

"That's only fair," the plant manager comments. Others express their agreement.

One cautious soul asks, "Are the measurements going to stay as they are now?"

"Not necessarily," answers Brian.

That stirs up a lot of uneasiness. Brian immediately reacts. "Let's discuss what measurement would make the most sense. Scott?"

Scott steps forward. "On the table there are two things that are important: immediate delivery and inventory. How would you suggest measuring the delivery performance?"

Several people suggest the method Pierco currently uses. "Number of orders not shipped."

"That could be an answer," Scott responds. "However, I personally have two minor problems with it. The first one is that according to that crude measurement, missing a shipment of an order of one hundred dollars is equal to missing an order of ten thousand dollars. I don't think that they're equal. I think that the measurement should consider the dollar value of the order missed. What do you think?"

This seems to make sense to everybody. "The other minor point is that the current measurement doesn't take into account by how much the order was late. Missing an order by one day is not as damaging as missing an order by a whole week."

Once again everybody agrees. "So what we see is that the measurement should consider both time and money. What is suggested is to measure late shipments by their dollar value multiplied by the number of days the shipment is late. This measurement of delivery performance is called throughput-dollar-days. Does it make sense to you?"

They seem to like it.

Scott continues. "The other important thing is inventory. You are measuring it today according to its dollar value. I think that if we want to give the plant full autonomy to determine its inventory levels we should not ignore the time factor. The plant should not be judged just on the level of inventory it holds, but also on how fast the inventory is moving. My suggestion is to use the inventory-dollar-days measurement. Multiplying the value of inventory by the number of days it stays under the plant responsibility."

Brian continues, "The plants prime measurement will then be to try to reach zero throughput-dollar-days. The secondary measurement is to do it with as few inventory-dollar-days as possible."

The noise level rises as people discuss it. Scott and Brian do not interfere for a long while.

Finally, Brian asks for quiet. "Well?"

One of the plant managers says, "We can live with it. Actually, we like it. It's logical and fair."

The warehouse manager from Kentucky raises his hand. "I have a problem," he states. "Why are you suggesting it only for the plants? Why can't we, the warehouse managers, get the same terms?"

He gains vocal support from all sides as he continues. "Let us also determine our inventory levels. We can do it much better than corporate." Raising his voice above the cheers he adds, "And yes, we are willing to be judged by the same measurements."

"Scott, can the computer system support it?" Brian asks.

"Sure."

Brian waits until it is quiet again and calmly says. "It's an excellent idea. So let's see what we are suggesting. We are talking about switching from push to pull. Each plant will have a plant warehouse. Replenishment from the plant to each regional warehouse will be done on a daily basis. The divisional headquarters will give everyone the best forecast they have about market trends, and information about upcoming marketing campaigns, but they will no longer determine the target inventory level. Instead, each manager in charge of a plant or a warehouse will have the authority to determine their own targeted inventory levels. But they will also be responsible for the results as measured by throughput-dollar-days and inventory-dollar-days."

Craig, Pierco's CEO, joins them on the stage. Brian unclips the microphone and passes it to him.

"Thank you Scott and thank you, Brian," Craig says. "What a performance." He starts to applaud and everybody joins in.

Scott and Brian clear the stage and Craig continues. "Fine. Ladies and gentlemen, I think that we have some important decisions to make. As we speak, inventories continue to climb, so we don't have the luxury of discussing it forever.

"Rooms are assigned for each division. You have tremendous experience. You have tremendous expertise. Discuss it among yourselves until you reach a binding decision. You have many options. You can decide to move on what we heard here. You can decide to do drastically different things. What I care about is that each division decide on an effective way to stop the accumulation of inventory. By the end of the day I want answers from each division. See you here at five P.M."

Chapter 18

MAY 3, 1999

Gail swivels away from her computer and twists her head and shoulders, trying to release the tension in her neck. She glances at her watch. Four hours have passed and she hadn't even noticed. This morning she had felt terrific. She had almost bounced from her car into the building. Now, looking at the document she just finished composing, she feels even better.

She taps out a message for Scott, attaches the document, and e-mails it. Scott will never believe it. Not coming from her.

Standing up, she stretches. Her meeting with Scott is not until one o'clock. She has just enough time to grab some lunch in the cafeteria. No, today she deserves better than that. They've opened a nice-looking deli three blocks away. Time to check it out.

Mary-Lou puts her phone call on hold and glances at her watch. "Hey, Gail. I was looking all over for you, go right in."

"Gail, great. This is great!" Scott stands up. "Want some coffee?"

"No thanks," she replies. "So what do you think?"

"I don't know what to think anymore. I never thought I'd see the day that you, on your own initiative, would up the sales forecast. And by so much?" Scott rubs his hands together, eyes sparkling.

"Perfect timing," he says. "Perfect. Actually, Gail, for the past two days I've been busy preparing a whole stack of arguments to convince you to commit to a modest increase."

"Pity I didn't know it." Gail smiles at him. "I'm sure that some of your arguments were in the form of increased bonuses for my people, or maybe options. Those are the best arguments for salespeople, you know."

"I know," Scott smiles back. "Hefty bonuses, huge commissions, and you blew it all." More seriously he adds, "Still, Gail, what caused you to raise the forecast for this year by over two hundred million a quarter?" Narrowing his eyes he asks, "Is there something I don't know?"

"Not really. You know what happened at Pierco, it was you who saved our skin there. Well, the whole incident upset Maggie to the extent that she decided not to allow it ever to happen again. That was enough."

"Gail, I understand every word you're saying. I think I even understand each sentence. But I definitely don't understand what you're talking about. I must be getting old."

Gail raises one eyebrow. "You? Old?" And in a factual tone she starts to explain. "You know the strategy that Maggie and I have adopted since the beginning of the year. Since some of our competitors became shaky we have targeted their clients, especially those clients that have not yet finished implementing. Rather than trying to convince them to throw away the competitors' ERP package and adopt ours, which probably no one would have agreed to, we offered to implement a part they hadn't yet installed. We offered our new production software, and promised unbelievable results in a very short time. This offer is very, very tempting. Many companies agreed to a pilot. We have our foot in the door."

"I know all that," Scott says impatiently. "In the first quarter, how many doors have we succeeded in getting our foot in? Almost a hundred, if I'm not mistaken."

"Yes. Do you also know that by April many of them had already increased their production to all-time record highs? You do. So after what you did at Pierco, Maggie decided that she's not going to let any of them blame us for ruining their cash flow. She insisted we approach each of the pilot plants that feed warehouses and had already increased their capacity. After we approached the first few I tried to stop her, but did you ever try to stop Maggie?"

"Talk about mission impossible! But Gail, why did you try to stop her?"

"Because she was too successful," Gail answers flatly. "She orchestrated it masterfully. Before the clients even noticed that their inventory was going up, KPI's account manager used the client's data to point out the trend of the inventories. Once the reason for it was explained, the client didn't have any grudge against us. Then it was no problem to arrange a day-long meeting, with all the relevant people, to present the Theory of Constraints application for distribution."

"I'm sure the trust is there and the pressure is there. So you got a one-day presentation. By the way, who plays my role and who plays Brian's?"

"No, Scott, nobody can play you. Our one-day presentations are much more conventional. First, the TOC expert on the account puts them in groups of three to play on a distribution simulation. I don't know where they got it, but it's a marvelous tool to convey both the magnitude of the problem and the power of the simple solution. You should see the participants after the session. Talk about conviction! Then, one of our guys presents the software, and then the KPI account manager constructs, with them, the next steps."

"Which are?"

"That's where it gets really interesting. To implement the distribution solution we must offer to replace the competitors' order-entry module and the measurement module. As you can imagine, we are only too happy to do that. Well, in half the cases the clients agreed, on the spot, to a sizeable pilot."

"Very nice." Scott is pleased. "Piloting such a big chunk of the ERP system, and with the bottom-line results, doesn't leave the competition much chance. It's just a matter of time until such a sizeable pilot will turn into a full implementation."

"Correct. But don't you want to hear what's happening in the other half of the cases?" Gail teases.

"You mean there's more? Of course, what I've heard so far wouldn't have caused you to increase the sales forecast. Okay, Gail, let's hear the full story. What's happening in the other half?"

"Well, it takes some more negotiations, but we've closed, or are about to close, contracts to install our entire package for the whole company. That's the problem."

"What problem?"

"I mean, that's what forced me to revise the forecast. In the forecast we did last December I was hoping that the pilots would expand toward the end of the year. As it is now, I can't possibly postpone enough even to the third quarter. The pressure to bring the inventories back under control is so high that these clients don't want to hear about any postponement. They insist on starting ASAP. So, some major contracts that I planned to work on toward the end of the year are closing this quarter."

"What about next quarter?"

"Scott, you're forgetting the number of pilots that are still in the works, and those that we keep on launching! The pipeline for the next quarter, and the one after that, is overflowing. I must admit, you were right, there is nothing more convincing to our clients than bottom-line results. Fast and hefty."

Scott, true to his nature, asks, "Gail, do you see anything that can stop us?"

"Stop us, no. Slow us down, yes. The software seems to be working well, and Maggie manages to always have enough good, experienced implementers. But finding TOC experts is turning into a nightmare."

"That's a concern," Scott agrees. "These TOC ideas may be basic and seem like common sense, but it's probably because they are so basic that proper education is necessary, mandatory, for people to change the rules. And changing the rules is key to the success of our implementations. Good TOC experts are vital."

"You don't have to convince me," Gail agrees. "But Scott, there simply aren't enough knowledgeable people available. And some of those who claim to be experts . . . well, they're not."

"In my attempts to learn as much as I can about TOC, I've met a few charlatans," Scott chuckles, "and that's putting it mildly!"

Gail continues seriously. "We need more TOC experts. Many more."

"I'm sure Maggie can come up with plenty of people. She's amazing at finding the best, and lots of them."

"You're wrong Scott. There aren't enough of them to find. We have to help to create them. I think you and Maggie need to join forces on this. Between the two of you, you can convince the best group of TOC experts to stop spending all their time in implementations, and switch their focus to teaching more experts. No matter how much it costs, not having enough TOC experts will cost us more."

"Okay, Gail. You're right. This is important. I'll talk to Maggie. Anything else that can slow us down?"

"There might be. But first, let me ask you a question. You said you were about to press me to raise the sales forecast. Why? What's wrong with the forecast we submitted at the beginning of the year?"

"Nothing," Scott answers. "But I knew that things were going better than we all expected, and the opportunity is simply to good to miss."

"What opportunity?"

"The opportunity to establish ourselves as the dominant ERP company. The leader. A breed apart."

Gail waits for him to continue.

"You know that last quarter only two of our competitors made their forecast."

Gail nods.

"Do you see them offering the market anything new?"

"No." Gail starts to smile in appreciation. "I'd say that they're scrambling. They're now offering deals they wouldn't have considered last year. And we are the only ERP supplier who raised its forecast for last quarter."

"And we met it," Scott declares. "We've gotten the attention of the analysts. Now imagine their reaction when, against the background of our competitors' floundering, we raise our forecast again."

Gail's smile widens. "We are going to be declared as the winner. We'll be the only show in town. What publicity! The kind money can't buy. Scott, you know what? With such a dominant position in the market, we won't have any problem winning most of the open bids." Grinning, she adds, "Before the end of the year, I'll have to revise the forecast again. So when are you going to announce our new forecast."

"You know how Wall Street analysts hate to be caught with their pants down. Now's the best time. It's early in the quarter, enough time to allow them to revise their evaluation of our company."

"It's great," Gail is bubbling. "Right when I opened my eyes this morning I knew it was going to be a gorgeous day."

"It is," says Scott. "Actually, so far it's a gorgeous year."

After a pause he inquires, "Gail, you said that there might be something else that could get in our way. What is it?"

"I'm in such a good mood, why ruin it? We'll discuss it some other time."

"And leave me hanging? Come on, Gail, you know how paranoid I am. Talk. I want to sleep tonight."

Gail is uncomfortable. "It's the communication that we have. Actually, the lack of communication." She stops.

After a moment, Scott encourages her. "Come on, this is serious. Such things can break a company. Who's not communicating?"

Gail swallows. "Scott, it's you."

Scott's expression doesn't reveal his surprise, nor how deeply he is hurt, but Gail knows him well enough to guess. She also knows that now she can't stop, she has to explain.

"Scott," she says softly, "with Pierco, I'll be the first one to admit that you and Lenny saved our company. It was brilliant. And now we have the best product we've ever had. But Scott, the way you did it was, allow me to say it, not the proper way. You put me, and even more so, Maggie, through hell.

"We were convinced that everything was ruined while you, correction, you and Lenny, were sitting on the solution. As we found out later, all the code was finished. And you didn't tell us about it. Not a word, no warning, no clue. You waited until it blew up in our face, until our best reference was threatening us, and only then did you say not to worry. Why? Why? I might expect such an attitude from Lenny, but from you?"

Scott's eyes soften when he says, "And now you're afraid there might be some more surprises up my sleeve . . ."

"Wouldn't you be? I know that Lenny is working on new things, but I don't have a clue what they are. In the past I was informed about every new development, on everything of importance cooking in our development centers. Not anymore."

She swallows hard and continues, "Scott, what's the next explosion going to be? You're so busy developing the solution, there must be something."

"You're right, Gail. You are absolutely right. I am guilty of not making the effort to communicate. So what do we do now?"

"We communicate." Gail sends a small smile. "But not now. Maggie should be part of it."

"Of course."

"What about tonight? Is eight okay?" she asks.

"No problem. But are you sure that Maggie's available?"

"She is in town, and for this, she'll be there."

Chapter 19

It's five after eight when Lenny enters Scott's office. Gail and Maggie are standing near one of the big windows. Scott is behind his desk.

"Hey Lenny," Scott greets him. "Ladies, we can start."

When they're all seated together, Scott says to Lenny, "It looks like we're not doing a good enough job of communicating."

"I agree," says Lenny.

Gail throws him a surprised look. Scott continues, "Gail and Maggie want to be kept informed on what's cooking in your development centers."

"It's about time," Lenny says harshly. "I send literature. I send documentation. I've tried everything except running naked in the corridors to draw attention. But it looks like everybody is too busy to notice." His voice gets deeper as he continues. "In a week or two all the code will be ready and we don't have a test site yet."

"What are you talking about?" Gail asks with irritation.

"What am I talking about?" Lenny repeats her words. "Don't you even read what I send you?"

"What is there to read?" Gail retorts. "In the past two months I haven't received a thing from you. Except more baloney on the Internet fad. As if I don't read the newspaper. Lenny, we are up to our ears with work. I don't need my mailbox filled with technical stuff about the Internet."

Lenny is about to explode. "You're calling my updates technical baloney?"

Gail doesn't answer. Scott puts his hand on Lenny's shoulder to stop him.

Looking at Gail, he reminds her, "We agreed that we need to work on improving the communication."

When no one comments, he continues. "While you and Maggie were doing an admirable job in the field, Lenny and I were working on the next steps. We were trying to anticipate our competitors' next moves. They're not going to just sit there, letting us take the entire market from them."

"What can they do?" Maggie speaks for the first time. "I don't believe that they can bring themselves to do what we do."

"I agree," Scott says. "But there are other things they can do."

Before he can continue, Gail interrupts. "Why are we so sure that they can't copy us? True, we caught them by surprise, but they're not dumb and they're not blind. They can see that what we're doing works. I'm sure that within the next few weeks many will announce that they too have the same software."

"Maybe so," Maggie answers. "But Gail, we discussed it several times, it's not just the software, it's the frame of mind."

Scott nods in agreement. "I agree with Maggie. The shift in paradigm that we decided on last December is much too big for most software companies to swallow."

"We switched from selling technology to selling value." Lenny puts in his two cents.

The last remark almost causes Gail to lose control. "For heaven's sake, you don't have to remind me of the slogan of my own marketing campaign."

Swallowing hard, she continues in a calmer voice. "I still think that we should not be fooled by our own words. Since when did we stop selling technology? We never stopped. We sell software. That's what we charge for. And as for selling value, please, give me a break. We didn't just start selling value this year; we've sold value all along. Don't tell me that the software we've been selling all these years was not bringing value, that companies bought it for no reason. Marketing slogans are nice, but let's leave them out of this room."

"Gail," Maggie says, "it's not just an empty slogan. It is the essence of what we did."

"Here we go again," Gail sighs, discouraging her from continuing.

Scott is shocked. Until this afternoon he was under the impression that the communication between the four of them was good. That they were all working from the same base. Nothing in the last few months gave him reason to suspect anything else. Their actions seemed to be in perfect synchronization. True, Gail may have her problems with Lenny, but that is to be expected when one deals with such different and strong personalities.

This afternoon he understood from Gail that there is something deeper then the usual friction, but only now does he realize how deep it is. Gail's last words reveal that she is not even on the same page.

What caused such a breakdown in communication?

Quickly Scott realizes that it is his fault. He didn't bother sharing his insight about what it takes for technology to bring value. He took it for granted. To the extent that since he spoke with Lenny about it, months ago, he never mentioned it to anybody. He decides to rectify it right now.

"Gail," Scott begins in a soft voice, "you're right that we still sell technology. And you're also right that we always sold things of value."

"Of course," says Gail. "ERP systems bring a lot of value."

Scott agrees. "The value of the ERP comes from that fact that it diminishes limitations." Reacting to Gail's impatient expression he quickly adds, "Let me finish. What I'm going to say is important. At least, I think so.

"So, as I said, what ERP brings is the ability to do things that were not possible before. There were severe limitations on the amount of data that could be quickly transferred between different functions in an organization. And in cases where data was collected, there were also severe limitations on the ability to comfortably and quickly retrieve relevant information from the oceans of data.

"I know you know all that. It's what you've been preaching for the last who knows how many years. But Gail, did you ever think what an organization would be like if it didn't have ERP technology? I mean, how would an organization operate if data couldn't be quickly transferred? How would it operate with almost no real-time information?"

"Interesting question," Maggie remarks.

"Think about it." Scott is now talking not just to Gail, but to Maggie and Lenny as well. "To cope with these limitations, organizations had almost no choice but to adapt a mode of management that is based on 'do the best you can do within the area that you can see'; within your work-center, your department, your silo. Organizations had almost no choice but to adapt a mode of management that is based on local optima."

He waits for this to sinks in and then continues.

"To support any mode of management, many rules are needed. Some of them are formal rules, most are informal; the things people know they should and shouldn't do. Recently we've gained a lot of experience in production. Can you think of any examples of rules that are clearly focusing on local optima?"

"Local efficiencies," Gail replies immediately. "The desire to make every work center as efficient as possible. Including non-bottlenecks. You see, Maggie, after hearing our presentation so many times, something rubbed off on me."

Scott smiles at her and says, "More examples."

Maggie gives another. "Forcing large batches on non-bottle-necks, to save on set-ups. Even though it inflates the lead time and causes other orders to be late."

Lenny contributes his share. "Assembling things and later cannibalizing those same assemblies. Or buying expensive machines even though neither total cost nor sales are affected."

"We can go on and on," Gail says. "But what are you driving at?"

"The point is," Scott says, patiently "that until recently we didn't consider that we, as an ERP provider, had anything to do with these types of rules. Actually, if we ever considered our clients' rules, it was in order to integrate their rules, as they were, into our software. Am I right?"

"And in the process, complicating our software beyond comprehension," Maggie adds.

"Tell me about it," Lenny sighs.

Gail thinks about it. Finally she says, "You're right."

"So you see Gail? Our technology diminished major limitations, but until recently we ignored the rules that resulted from the existence of those limitations. We left them unchallenged. So what happened when we installed the technology and those rules were still used? Look at the new production implementations. Could we hope for such excellent results if the plants where still chasing local efficiencies and large batches?"

"Of course not," says Gail. "We have thousands of old implementations to prove it. Okay Scott, I see what you mean now. Removing the 'physical' limitations of technology is not enough. The limitations, even when removed, are still there; they are there because the rules keep them alive."

"Precisely," Scott confirms, pleased. "To realize value, bottom-line value, technology is necessary but not sufficient. Since the beginning of the year we have concentrated on bringing value. We no longer confine ourselves to just technology, we provide everything that is needed to get the potential value, even if it means doing things that a software company is not supposed to do."

"Like almost forcing the prospects to change their old management rules." Maggie completes his sentence.

"By the way," Lenny comments, "realizing what rules have to be changed does have an impact on our software. In many ways it simplifies the code, but it does necessitate some important additions. Buffer-management is an excellent example."

Gail thinks about it some more. "On one hand I see why you say that we switched to selling value. But on the other, it is not correct to say that we switched from selling technology, because we still sell technology."

After a second she adds, "Forget it. The important thing is that I still don't see what prevents our competitors from doing the same."

"Their mentality," Maggie answers decisively.

"Here we go again." Gail sounds disgusted. "If you want to convince me will you please use arguments, not slogans."

"It's not a slogan," Lenny says in a harsh tone. "Software engineers have the mentality of designing code with one purpose in mind: to impress everybody with the sophistication and sleekness of their software. The impact it has on the bottom line of the user is almost nonexistent for them. Take our APS module for example. I explained and explained why, in order for our users to get good results, we should optimize just the bottleneck. Still, do you know how many fights I had to go through to force them to take out the oversophistication? And do you know why? Because optimizing a hundred work-centers is by far more impressive than optimizing just one or two."

"APS is a special case," Gail says.

Lenny doesn't accept it. "Special case?" he sneers. "Fine, what about distribution? Most of the changes didn't require writing more code, but erasing huge chunks of the existing code. You should have seen what a fight they put up. I almost gave up."

"Good thing you didn't," says Maggie.

"Thank you."

"So, Lenny," Scott says, "you are of the opinion that this

mentality will block our competitors from catching up with us?"

"No way. Even if we give them our code then, I bet that within few weeks, they will sophisticate it out of usability."

When it comes to programming Gail has full respect for Lenny's opinions. No wonder that his conviction has a real impact on her.

She is still assessing it when Maggie breaks into her thoughts. "What Lenny said is correct, but I was thinking about the implementors' mentality."

"What do you mean?" Lenny asks.

"The mentality of ERP implementors is to start in the areas where the technology is most needed, where massive volumes of data have to be gathered and distributed. That means that we used to start the implementations with either the financial or the order-entry modules. The last thing that was implemented was plant scheduling and control. Now that our focus is on bringing bottom-line results, we have to do the exact opposite. We start in production and distribution.

"I know how difficult it is for them to adjust. We have problems with every new group of experienced implementors that we contract. My project managers have to practically force them to do it right, and they bitch and moan, at least until the results are clearly there."

"And what about the mentality of the salespeople?" Scott asks.

Gail doesn't answer. That provokes Maggie to say, "Listen Gail, until this year, how did we persuade companies to buy? We did everything to impress them with our technology. The value part was nothing more than just lip service; look at what we called 'business justification?' It was a joke; most of the items were not even related to the bottom line. Have you forgotten what the vocabulary of your salespeople was? It was all configurations and features."

"Unfortunately, to a large extent it still is," Gail admits. "I'm sure that we lost a few excellent opportunities due to it."

"More than just a few." Maggie is in high gear. "And we would have lost many more if not for the structured presentations we imposed on our people . . . And for the fact that we invested so much in their re-orientation . . . And for the fact that in the sales process we involved a TOC expert early on. These people know nothing but bottom-line value, the software they regard as a necessary evil."

Gail feels the need to protect her people. "What do you expect when we turn everything around? It takes time to adjust."

"Precisely my point." Maggie rests her case. "A lot of time."

"Switching from selling just technology," Scott summarizes, "to selling value needs the synchronized change in all functions, system engineers, salespeople and implementors. On top of it a new function must be introduced, the change agent, the TOC expert. This is why I'm not afraid that our competitors will soon catch up. We have just started to open a significant competitive edge. Gail, do you agree?"

"Yes, I do. I'm now convinced that it will not be easy for them to close the gap. But Scott, why do you say that we have just started? What else are you planning for us?"

"Nothing to be afraid of," he smiles in assurance. "We are over the hump. But there is still a lot to be done. Let's not forget that our ERP covers all aspects of an organization, not just production and distribution. And what we've said holds true everywhere. If we don't bother to change the inappropriate rules, our technology is not going to bring all the benefits it is capable of."

Maggie and Gail nod in appreciation.

Scott continues. "Locating which rules are based on local optima is not a trivial task. Finding appropriate new rules is even harder. Just ask Brian how difficult it was to find the correct rules for distribution. He tried everything—changing the plants' measurements, changing the targeted levels—and it was far from sufficient. We were lucky, unbelievably lucky, that all this work was already done. Just waiting for us to capitalize on."

"You mean the body of knowledge of the Theory of Constraints?" Maggie asks.

"Of course," Scott replies. "So, as you know, I started by studying everything and anything that I could about TOC, while Lenny turned his attention to an area in which we had very little to offer, engineering."

"Where do we stand on the engineering module?" Gail asks.

"Whenever you want it, it's ready," Lenny answers. "We tested it. It's excellent. Actually, all our development work is now planned and controlled by this application. It makes a big difference; we are able to develop almost twice as much in half the time. But Gail, other companies are already offering Critical Chain software."

"Yes, I know," she says. "But is our module ready?"

"Yes," he answers. "Regular progress reports were sent to you. And you should be getting the manual this week. Make sure it doesn't block your mailbox," he adds sarcastically.

Before Gail has a chance to snap back, Scott says, "My first priority was to complete our package for the entire supply chain. Production we had. Engineering, Lenny was working on. So I started studying distribution. By the end of January, I was able to pass the information to Lenny. He picked up the ball and ran with it. Lucky for us, otherwise we would have been in a deep hole by now."

"You can say that again," Maggie shivers. Then angrily she turns to Lenny. "You jerk. You were sitting on the solution not saying a word. Not even when George called you, begging for help."

"But Maggie," Lenny is almost desperate, "what do you want from me? You were informed about our distribution module. You were sent full documentation, I checked. We even got comments from your people."

"So how come you didn't want to help George?" Maggie is still on the warpath.

"Come on, Maggie." Lenny starts to become irritated. "George didn't say a word about distribution. He just talked about the forecast module, demanding the impossible. How was I supposed to know that inventories were swamping Brain's warehouses?"

"It's my fault," Scott says softly. "I should have predicted it much before it became such a big problem. I knew that a change in rules in one function might have an impact on another function. I'm sorry, I was looking for a connection between the rules, and that was my mistake. I neglected to look at the impact, the impact that a sharp improvement in one function might have elsewhere."

"That's okay, Scott," Gail says softly, "In hindsight everybody has twenty-twenty vision. But what I'm worried about is the future. What similar things are we going to clash into in the future?"

"After the Pierco scare, you can imagine that I gave it a lot of thought. I have good news. So far I haven't come up with any other such devastating cases. It looks like from now on we are sailing in calm waters."

Gail is still not entirely relaxed. "So what's all the noise coming from Lenny's kingdom? What are they frantically developing there?"

"It's just that Internet stuff." Lenny gives her a diabolical grin. "Just trying to be one step ahead of the competition."

Gail looks at Scott.

"As we said earlier," Scott starts to explain, "we're not really worried about our competitors embarking on the value route. Not for a long while at least. So Lenny and I racked our brains to try and figure out what else they might do."

Lenny picks it up. "Being technology oriented, we thought that they would look for a super-duper technical solution. Something that would impress the market."

"And the Internet is the obvious answer," Maggie smiles at him.

"Of course. What is more natural than enabling the ERP to work over the Internet? What is better for our industry than a blend of advanced technology and a real business need? Of course, we have a unique approach. We don't look just at the technology, we also look at which rules acknowledge the limitation we are about to diminish. So I asked Scott to look into it. He came back with the 'trivial' answers and we wrote the code. You have it all in your mailbox, so don't ask me to repeat it here."

"Please don't," Scott chuckles. "If Lenny starts talking about it, we'll be here till morning. But we need a beta test. I was thinking of Pierco, they're the most advanced client we have. What do you think?"

"It's a natural choice," Gail agrees.

"And to Craig, you are second only to God," Maggie adds. "Whatever you want to implement in his company he will be more than willing to pay you for it. So you know what? Just to prevent you from using dirty words like beta test, let me read Lenny's documents and I'll prime Craig for you."

Chapter 20

"Hi, Scott."

Scott doesn't have any problem identifying the deep voice. "Hi, Craig, what's up? Any new problems?"

"So that's how you think of me? If I call, it must be problems." Craig's laughter is loud, even over the phone. "No, nothing of the sort. I'm passing through town, and I wonder if we can have dinner tonight?"

"Sure thing. But Craig, this is my town, so let me take care of the arrangements." Checking his day planner, Scott asks, "Seven-thirty?"

"That'll be perfect," Craig answers. "It would be nice if Maggie could join us too."

"I'm sure she'll be delighted," Scott assures him.

"Excellent. Will somebody call my secretary with the location? See you at seven-thirty."

Scott smiles as he presses Maggie's direct line.

"Maggie, you never cease to amaze me," he says. "You sure are one of a kind. How did you manage to pull it off?"

"Thanks for the compliment, but Scott, what are you talking about?"

"I'm talking about Craig."

"What about him?"

"You and I are having dinner with him tonight."

"Really? When? Where?"

"Seven-thirty, in a restaurant to be determined by Mary-Lou. Can you come?"

"Of course I'll come. What do you think? That I'd let the two of you get together without me?"

"I didn't think so. But tell me, how did you get him to come here? And on such a short notice?" In a more cautious voice he adds, "Maggie, what did you promise him?"

"Two new modules and half of Lenny's time." After a moment, Maggie laughs. "Just kidding. Scott, you give me too much credit. I didn't even speak with the man. All I did was send him a short write-up of your approach, something I scribbled after our meeting. You know, that technology is necessary but not sufficient, that kind of stuff."

"So why is he here?"

"I'm not sure. I also mentioned that we have something interesting coming up with Internet technology, but I didn't give any details."

"Fine, we'll find out for sure at seven-thirty. See you then."

"Wait, Scott. Can you transfer me to Mary-Lou? I want to make sure she selects the right restaurant. Fancy enough for Craig, a private room so we can talk business and, most important, with food I like."

They haven't finished the salad course when Craig shifts the conversation away from small talk. "I want to personally thank you for what you've done. These last changes are working beyond our expectations. Pierco is not the same company it was a year ago."

"Thank you," Scott says. "And thank you for being so cooperative about sharing it with our prospects."

"Yes," Maggie joins in. "And especially for allowing your

people to share actual numbers. That inventory drop is spectacular."

"All the tangible results are like that," Craig comments. "The increase in capacity, the reduction in response time, in cross shipments, in shortages. But for me the most impressive thing is what happened between the production and distribution managers. They used to be like wolves, always at each other's throats, always blaming each other."

"And now?" Scott asks.

"In the last four weeks none of the divisional managers got even a single complaint."

Scott nods in appreciation. "That's impressive. The first time I understood the dollar-days measurements I knew that they were powerful. But I had no idea that they were powerful enough to bring down the barriers between the production and distribution silos."

"Well, they are." Craig looks content. "At last I see real collaboration between different functions."

"I'm glad to hear it," Maggie says. "I'm also glad that it's over."

Craig puts his fork down and in his deep voice says, "That's what I came to talk about. It's not over. It's just the beginning."

Without noticing, both Maggie and Scott lean forward.

"What we have done so far is good but not good enough," Craig firmly states. "Pierco is now much more agile, but most of it doesn't reach the end customer. And as long as the end customer doesn't enjoy it, we aren't getting the biggest benefit, the lift in sales.

Maggie is confused. "Why doesn't it reach the end customer?"

"Maggie, we don't sell most of our products directly to the market. We sell to retail companies or to other manufacturers. Last month we ran some surveys. And these surveys clearly show that the fact that we significantly improved our deliveries to our client, didn't improve their delivery performance by much."

"I see," she says thoughtfully.

Craig continues. "Well, as you know, competition becomes more fierce every year. I think that the battlefield is changing. I think that the battles are actually fought, not so much between companies, but mainly between supply chains. And Pierco, as large as it is, is still just one link in a supply chain. If we want to win big we must look beyond the limits of our company. We must look on our entire supply chain."

"That's interesting," Maggie says. "How are you planning to do that?"

Craig waits until the waiter finishes serving the main dishes before he begins. "I want to extend what we've done to my entire supply chain; to my clients, my vendors, and their vendors. All the way from raw materials to the end customers. That's how we'll gain the competitive edge."

"That's a huge business to business project," Maggie states. "How many companies are in your supply chain? It must be in the hundreds." Her face lights up as she realizes the magnitude of the opportunity.

"Yes," Craig agrees. "The project is huge, but I believe that it's vital. What I want is not just to persuade them to implement the solutions for production and distribution but also . . ."

"The solution for engineering," Maggie jumps in, completing his sentence. "Being able to quickly develop and introduce new products is a major part of the equation."

Craig is surprised. "You have a way to shrink product development? Why didn't you tell me about it?"

"Because we're releasing it just next month," Scott explains. "We first wanted to complete the tests on our software development projects. But Craig, you were about to say something else."

Craig is eager to hear more, but he is also eager to move on with his agenda. After a second of hesitation he continues, "So as I said, I want to persuade every company in my supply chain to improve their operations. But that's not enough. I think that for the supply chain to reach its full potential, not just the links have to improve, but also the collaboration between the links has to be improved. The entire supply chain has to work as one unit. We succeeded in doing it with our plants and warehouses. There is no reason why we shouldn't succeed in doing the same between our company and the others in our supply chain."

"Craig," Scott says, "these two cases are not the same. Two departments of the same company, each trying to optimize their own local performance is stupid. But different companies, on the other hand, have to look out for their own bottom line."

Craig doesn't buy it. "If companies belong to the same supply chain, I claim that it's about time they realize that if the chain loses, every company in the chain loses. So it's not so different."

Scott and Maggie agree.

"Causing different companies to work as one unit is a tall order," Maggie remarks.

"You can say that again," Craig sighs. "Many CEOs have tried to get full collaboration from their vendors and clients. I don't know of any that really succeeded. And I'll be the first to admit that I don't know how to do it." He pauses and then states, "But Scott, Maggie told me that you know."

Maggie almost chokes on her food.

Craig continues. "Maggie, thank you for sending me that write-up of yours. It's so obvious that when we install new technology we also have to modify the related rules, yet we never do it. Until recently that is. So, when you informed me about your new development, the ability to link companies over the Internet, I understood that you were also working on modifying the rules that govern the collaboration between companies. Was I wrong?"

"You were right," Scott smiles.

Craig smiles back in relief. "So, tell me."

Scott takes a sip from his glass of red wine, and decides to start by stating the objective. "You want all the companies in the supply chain to act on the concept that the best way to guarantee success is to make sure that the chain is successful."

"Correct."

"Well, I believe, that even with the best intentions, this concept will remain an empty slogan until we'll change the day-to-day practice to match it. The current practice is almost the opposite."

Craig chews on another piece of his juicy steak while waiting for Scott to explain his broad claim.

"Suppose that I'm one of the companies in your chain. When do I register a sale? The minute I ship the goods to the next company in the chain. I've made a sale, but did the chain make a sale? No. You can see that the performance of the individual companies is not tied to the performance of the chain."

Craig swallows and says, "You're right for the short term. But companies also have to look at the long run. Suppose that I'm selling one hundred units per month to another company, and that company succeeds in selling only fifty units per month to its clients. Am I happy? Do I say, 'I'm selling them one hundred a month, I don't care how much they sell or use?' That would be very shortsighted of me. If they don't use what I sell them, soon I don't have a client."

"Correct," Scott agrees. "We have a contradiction here. The day-to-day practice is that a sale is done whenever a single link ships to the other. That is the opposite of the long-term business sense; a sale is done only when the last link in the chain has sold to the end customer. Craig, how many times have you seen the long-term interest dictating the behavior of people? Relative to how many times you have seen the day-to-day practice dictating it."

"I understand. You claim that we don't have a choice but to change the day-to-day practice," Craig concludes.

Scott declares, "If we want to see in our lifetime individual companies acting according to the good of their supply chain, I think that we should make sure that the day-to-day practice will match the long-term business sense."

Maggie says it explicitly. "The day-to-day practice should be:

as long as the end customer didn't buy, nobody in the supply chain has sold."

"Makes sense," Craig says slowly. "Makes perfect sense. But that won't be easy to implement. I don't think that my vendors will be happy to wait that long to get paid. To wait until, eventually, the end consumer buys. And you can't blame them, most don't have the hefty cash reserves needed for such a long delay in payment."

"Why do you claim that they'll have to wait much longer than now?" Maggie asks. "I'm sorry, but I was under the impression that you said you want to extend what you have done with our software to your entire supply chain. That's how you intend to get the competitive edge. How much have you reduced the lead time through Pierco? A quarter of what it was?"

"Less," Craig says.

"So," Maggie continues. "Suppose that the whole chain reaches comparable improvements. Then what will be the average lead time? From raw materials, which are commodities, until final sale? I would say, about two months. Not too bad considering that today your vendors have to wait a minimum of forty-five days for their money."

Craig thinks about it. "Still, for some of the upstream companies it will be too long to wait. We'll have to arrange some line of credit for them."

"Will it be a problem?" Maggie asks.

Craig doesn't see it as a big problem. "We are holding their inventories without paying for them. The least that we can do is to put up the collateral. Even my CFO will not have a problem with it. Besides, let's put things into perspective. The last improvements gave us excess capacity in both production and distribution. Our vendors and clients should get the same. Once they have that excess capacity, an increase in sales is not going to be associated with an increase in expenses. What is the bottom-line impact of having a competitive edge that will increase sales by, let's say, only ten percent? It's huge. In comparison, the small sums that will have to be paid for interest are less than peanuts."

They continue to eat, each absorbed in their own thoughts. After a minute Craig says, "Good. It does make sense. If I know that I'm not going to get paid until my client sells, then I will have his interests in mind. That will force the individual links to at last act as a chain."

He thinks about it some more and says, "I'm not sure that we'll stay with all the clients we currently have. I don't trust some of them to know what they're doing. I don't know if I want to give them my goods without being paid right away."

Craig now has a long face.

Scott doesn't help much when he says, "And judging Pierco based on last year's performance, some of your vendors might say the same."

Before Craig can comment he adds. "What you need is a good measurement. A measurement that will unequivocally tell you if your client is trustworthy. If when he asks for your goods he really needs them; if he is rapidly moving them to the market."

"Right!" Craig's face lights up again. "And I have the measurement. You gave it to me. Inventory-dollar-days. The situation is not much different than what we've done internally. Today we trust our plants and warehouses to determine the targeted inventories themselves. Those that just pad themselves with hefty stocks are flagged out by the inventory-dollar-days measurement like a sore thumb. This measurement is excellent for that. I can do the same with my clients. You want my inventory? I want to know the dollar-days value that you hold. And the companies that do not perform will not be our partners for long."

"The inventory-dollar-days enable a vendor to judge his client. You'll have to offer the same to your vendors so they can judge you," Maggie comments.

"Yes. The same terms that will be between us and our clients will also be between my vendors and us. It helps to have uniformity across the chain. But that also means that I'll ask from my vendors what I give to my clients. I'm holding inventory near my clients. I'm supplying whatever they want the same day. I want to get the same service."

"If that's what you want," says Scott, "if you are going to put such an emphasis on on-time deliveries, then you'll have to judge your vendors by the throughput-dollar-days.

"Of course," Craig replies. "Everyone will be measured not just by inventory-dollar-days but by throughput-dollar-days as well. Trust is nice as long as there are measurements that serve as a watchdog."

"That's nice," Maggie comments. "The same operational measurements inside each link and between the links. Craig, do you realize that what you are talking about here can only be done by the ERP of BGSoft?"

"I'm fully aware of that. By the way, can your software handle the additional requirements that we talked about here?" he asks.

"The code is ready," Scott answers.

"Ever tested?"

"Only in the laboratory," Scott admits.

"That's okay," Craig says, to Maggie's relief. "You'll have ample time to test it. There are hundreds of companies I'll have to convince. And I'm not going to start with them all at once. But regarding your software, there is a practical problem. And that is what I want to discuss with you."

The waiter approaches their table with the dessert trolley. Impatiently, Maggie selects dessert and orders coffee for them all. "What is the problem?" she asks.

"My vendors and clients all use different software packages; many of them are homegrown. It won't be easy to persuade them to switch to BGSoft."

"But is it possible?" Scott asks.

"It shouldn't be too difficult," Maggie says. "Unlike other large companies, you are approaching them after you yourself implemented what you are asking them to do. And you can show them the results. No one can ignore such results."

"Pierco is big enough," Craig answers, "to put pressure on all its vendors and most of its clients. But there is a limit. What I'm asking for must be reasonable."

"And it's unreasonable to ask them to change to the only ERP that can do it?" Maggie asks.

"Yes, Maggie, it's unreasonable. The few that are large companies have already invested a lot of money and effort to implement other ERP systems. They won't be eager to throw it away. And the majority are medium to small companies that simply don't have the resources to implement your software. Not the money or the manpower."

"It's a big obstacle," Scott agrees.

After a moment of silence, Craig responds with a straight face, "It's not so big, if you're willing to change as well."

Maggie says sharply, "Don't even suggest we do it for free, or almost for free. I know all the arguments and I'm telling you it will not work."

"Maggie, I know you better than to even think about it," Craig assures her. He signals to the waiter. "I'd like an after dinner drink. How about you?"

"Trying to get us drunk?" Maggie jokes. "Yes, please, I'd like an Irish coffee."

"Cognac for me," says Scott.

Once the waiter is on his way to the bar, Craig starts. "Maggie, investing two or three hundred million dollars is almost routine for Pierco, but I still know how difficult it was for me to decide on a new ERP system. You know why? Because investing in computer systems is not like investing in anything else. It's not like investing in a new company or like investing in a building or a machine. You put out so much money and what do you have in your hands? Nothing you can resell, nothing you can offer as collateral. It wasn't easy for me and it won't be any easier for my vendors. So I was wondering, what offer could you make to a company that would bring no less money to you but would made their decision much easier?"

"That's an interesting approach," Scott says.

"Carry on," Maggie says.

"Over the last three years I paid, to both your companies, about three hundred million dollars. And I'll still continue to pay, for maintenance and such, about ten million a year. But you know what? I would gladly pay you a hundred million a year, forever, if I didn't have to buy your software and the implementation." He stops.

"What would you pay a hundred million a year for?" Maggie is all ears.

"For doing exactly what you did. Well, maybe a little bit more. If you agreed to subcontract all my computer related logistics, I would be happy to pay you that much. You handle the data; my people will enter it, but you handle it. You make sure that my people have the information they need. Your computers, your software—I don't want to know about them. I don't want to hear about bugs. I don't want to hear about new versions. I don't want to hear about new hardware. That's your headache. What I want are the end results. The information available when my people need it, where they need it, and in whatever form they need it."

Maggie and Scott look at each other. For a while nobody moves. Finally Maggie nods, and Scott says, "You know Craig, a year ago I would have considered your offer ridiculous."

"Why?"

"Because it would guarantee that BGSoft would go out of business."

"Why?"

"If a client can ask for whatever he wants without paying for it, he will never stop asking for changes; for new features, for new modules, for new templates, for whatever. As a matter of fact, clients are asking for those things even when they do have to pay for them. So, we would have faced two alternatives. Either do what the clients want and go out of business, or upset the clients and go out of business. But with Pierco, at this point, I'll consider it."

"What's the difference? Are we so unique?"

"You became unique. Craig, since you started working according to TOC, requests for changes coming from your company have dropped to a small fraction of what they were before. And the requests we get are not because of a whim, they make sense. You see, in Pierco, what drives the system now is very different from before. Every request is justified by bottom-line argument. What a world of difference it makes. Maggie, do you agree?"

"I do, and I'm sure Lenny will. But Scott, the real reason is that previously people were operating under conflicting measurements. How can you strive for high local efficiencies while you have to lower inventories and lead time? And the joke is that they thought they could get a better answer if the computer would just do that . . . and that . . . and that . . . That's why they constantly asked for changes."

"You're right, Maggie. Absolutely right. So Craig, we might entertain your suggestion, but only for companies that agree up front that they will adopt the holistic approach of TOC. Everything is judged by the impact on the bottom line, short-term as well as long-term. And to hell with local optima."

"Scott, you're bursting through an already open door. We already said that. To be a valuable member of the supply chain, companies will have to adopt what we have done. Those are the companies that I'm concerned about, and I'm willing to work on that closely."

Maggie nods, and asks them both, "What about the small companies? How much do you think they can pay?"

Craig has already thought about all these points. "The same as Pierco," he answers. Seeing Maggie's puzzled look, he hurries to explain. "I mean, in relative terms. One hundred million is one percent of Pierco's yearly turnover. It should not be a problem to convince the others to pay the same. One percent of turnover. Actually, today they probably pay more to get what you'll deliver. Well, will you do it?"

"Craig, I hope you don't expect an answer right now," Maggie says.

"I'm not expecting an answer immediately. But when can I get an answer? You understand that it is key to my entire supply chain strategy."

"Craig, my first impression is good," Maggie answers. "What you are suggesting has the potential to solve a large problem for us. I've been racking my brain for a long time to figure out a way to avoid the problem of exhausting our market. The way we currently do business, we constantly have to expand to new clients. Your idea will solve this problem completely. It turns a one-shot deal into a constant stream of income. A big one. It can give us incredible stability." After a short pause she adds, "And Scott, for the long run, it will increase even your rate of growth. What do you think?"

"Maggie, it will increase our rate of growth even in the short run," Scott answers. "Craig's suggestion has another big advantage. It gives us, at last, a way to really capitalize on the medium-sized-company market. For years we've wondered how to economically penetrate this huge market. What we are now talking about is using the sizeable base we have in the large companies as a lever to enter the mid- and small-sized companies."

"A lever?" laughs Craig. "A bulldozer! If we push for it, gently, just announcing that Pierco prefers doing business with companies that take our sensible offer, and if we do justice to our win-win offer by explaining it clearly, without hiding a thing, how many of our vendors, and clients, do you think will agree?"

"A lot. The majority."

Craig now repeats his question. "Can I get an answer in, let's say, two weeks?"

Scott is uncomfortable. "Craig, this would be a drastic change in the way we do business. For both BGSoft and KPI.

Still, I must admit that if we think about it for more than just five minutes and do not find any real showstopper, then I think we gained much more from this dinner than you did. The phenomenal growth rate we're enjoying this year will be a snail's pace in comparison to what I can now envision. But let me stress, that's *if* there are no showstoppers. *If* there is not something, that right now we don't see, that makes this idea too risky."

Seeing that Craig intends to continue to press, Maggie says, "These are things we have to discuss with our people. It will take much more than two weeks before we can come up with a definite answer. Three to six months is more likely."

Craig doesn't seem surprised. "Okay," he says. "But maybe you can give me a quicker answer on another question. I want you to supply Pierco with this service. But we of course have already paid for the software and the vast majority of the implementation, so how about the following offer? Pierco will pay you, and I mean a joint venture of both your companies, half a percent a year of our turnover until the total sum reaches the amount we have already paid you. Then it jumps to one percent a year."

"Are you serious?" Maggie asks, her eyes glittering.

Rather than answering, Craig opens his briefcase and hands a copy of a proposal to each of them.

Scott and Maggie both know that they are hooked. The offer is simply too good to turn down.

"I'll patiently wait for your answer," Craig says, smiling.

THE END
or just
THE BEGINNING

ABOUT THE AUTHORS

Eli Goldratt is the creator of the Theory of Constraints and the author of the mega-bestsellers *The Goal, It's Not Luck* and *Critical Chain*.

Carol A. Ptak is a leading authority in the use of ERP and Supply Chain tools to drive improved bottom line performance, Ms. Ptak's expertise is well grounded in over two decades of practical experience as a successful practitioner, consultant and educator in manufacturing operations. Her pragmatic approach to complex issues and dynamic presentation style have her in high demand worldwide on the subject of how to leverage these tools and successfully become an e-business. Ms. Ptak is the President and CEO of APICS, The Educational Society for Resource Management for the year 2000 and is employed by IBM as a Program Director for Mid-Market solutions.

Eli Schragenheim is one of the pioneers of TOC and is recognized as an authority in ERP related simulations. He has published several papers in academic and practitioner journals and has delivered hundreds of workshops for managers. He is a frequent speaker at international conferences in the US, UK and Israel, on topics concerning TOC, learning from experience and information systems in operations.